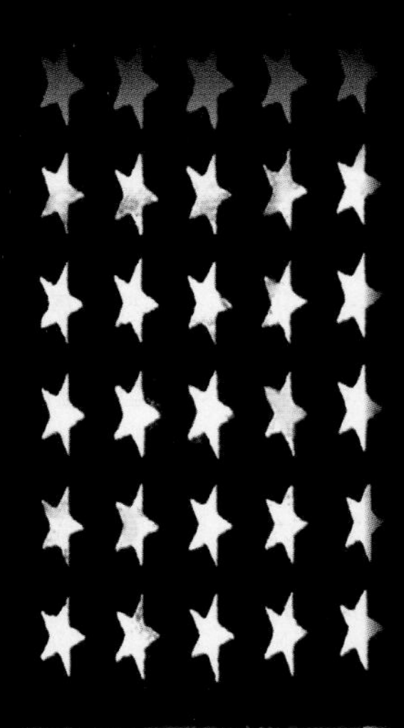

Rayc

AMERICANA PRICE GUIDE

The premiere source for the antiques and collectibles market

VOLUME ONE

COLLECTOR BOOKS
A Division of Schroeder Publishing Co., Inc.

Front cover:
Silk American flag, Early 1940s, strong demand, 8/10 rarity, $150.00 – 160.00.
Pillow cover, 1920 – early 1940s, strong demand, 8/10 rarity, $135.00 – 160.00.
10" Doughboy Tank, appeared in the late 1930s – early 1940s, $300.00.
Short-stem rooster, Hummer rooster, Elgin Wind & Power, $1,000.00 – 1,200.00.
Rare peach with carved marble pit, 1880 – 1910, $1,500.00 – 1,800.00.
Back cover:
Rare Babe Ruth check made out to Cadillac in 1936, $4,000.00 – 5,000.00.

Cover design by Beth Summers
Book design by Barry Buchanan

COLLECTOR BOOKS
P.O. Box 3009
Paducah, Kentucky 42002-3009
www.collectorbooks.com

20.00

The current values in this book should be used only as a guide. They are not intended to set prices, which vary from one section of the country to another. Auction prices as well as dealer prices vary greatly and are affected by condition as well as demand. Neither the authors nor the publisher assumes responsibility for any losses that might be incurred as a result of consulting this guide.

Searching For A Publisher?

We are always looking for knowledgeable people considered to be experts within their fields. If you feel that there is a real need for a book on your collectible subject and have a large comprehensive collection, contact Collector Books.

Contents

Dedication

For ELR, who persevered for 89 years with generosity and patience for her son and three grandsons.

Acknowledgments

The authors appreciate the contributions of the individuals and couples who have made this project a positive experience.
Phil & Mary Lynn Edwards
Bob & Judy Farling
Donna Vaughan
Chuck "Sonny" Conner
Ralph Dunbar
Chris Fricker Auctions
Bill Bunn
Bloomington, Illinois, Antiques Mall
Dutch Hagenbruch
Raymond Gerdes
Dr. Ben Gentry
Carlene & Ken Elliott
3rd Sunday Market
Col. Edgardo Adriano (U.S.N. Ret.)
Katherine & Elizabeth Raycraft
Aumann Auctions
Jack Bazzani
Captain Alex Hood
Dale & Vonnie Troyer
John Cunningham & family
Carol & Emily Raycraft

Preface

My late mother had a theory that there were "golden moments" in life when you had only an instant to jump on the bus or it would unfailingly go on to the next stop without you. You could wait on that corner forever but, you would never see that particular bus again.

When Cal Ripken Jr. broke Lou Gehrig's record for playing in consecutive baseball games (more than 2,100) I felt he missed an absolute golden moment. Gehrig was an icon in the Hall of Fame for positive role models, as is Ripken.

My thought was that Ripken should have tied the Gehrig record and not have surpassed it. This would have shown respect to Gehrig and a record that will never again be approached. Ripken matches the record and sits out the next game, but as is usually the case, the golden moment was missed.

As antique collectors, my wife and I have had periodic golden moments. Some we grasped and others we missed for a variety of reasons. Before there is a golden moment, you have to comprehend that, in fact, it is a golden moment. This takes awareness and knowledge.

On February 15, 1985, we received a note from a dealer who had a collection of windmill weights for sale. There were 32 weights offered for a total of $5,000.00.

#2 Long tail horse - 2
#4 Short tail horse - 10
#11 Challenge Spear - 1
#16 Fairbury Bull - marked - 1
#17 Fairbury Bull - unmarked - 4
#22 Unmarked Boss Bull - 1
#27 Hummer - 4
#42 W - 2
#53 Buffalo
#65 Star - 1
#91 Dry Eclipse
#92 Eclipse -
#93 Eclipse -
#94 Eclipse -
Price for all $5000

Preface

The number at left of the weight correlates with numbers assigned by Sites in his book, *Windmills and Windmill Weights.* The book was initially offered in 1977 and became a primary resource for dealers and collectors in communicating exactly what was available. For example: the dealer who offered us the weights had 10 short-tailed horses (identified in the book as #4), one buffalo (#53), four unmarked Fairbury bulls (#17), and 17 other weights for the $5,000.00 plus postage.

The golden moment, like its name implies, was fleeting. We missed it but we have not forgotten it and it still comes up in periodic moments of stress.

The point of the above narrative is that you need to be aware and have the knowledge to jump on the bus and seize the moment. An old time dealer told us almost 40 years ago, "The money is always easier to get than the stuff."

He and my mother were both right.

Don Raycraft
Fall 2005

In the April 14, 2005, edition of the *New York Times* there is a heavily illustrated advertisement from ABC Carpet & Home in New York City. ABC is one of the great "home" stores in the world with floors of diverse furnishings from across the globe.

On multiple trips to China and Tibet I have noticed a growing amount of antique (by our standards) and used furniture (by the local citizenry). As the Chinese economy evolves, furnishings handed down for six or seven generations in rural areas are being replaced by mail-order tables, chairs, and cupboards that are more fashionable than what has been in daily use for 150 years. By Chinese standards the used furniture has no value. Pickers come to the rural areas and buy truckloads, as other trucks deliver the catalogue merchandise that will decorate the homes of a growing middle class of consumers.

The advertisement from ABC Carpet and Home offered recycled tapestries for seat covers on chairs and couches, reclaimed teak tables, and vintage rugs.

A number of antiques and collectibles puveyers feel that the future of selling "Americana" may begin in the villages of rural China, Nepal, and Tibet. Words like "recycled," "vintage," and "reclaimed" will become more prevelant on price tags at shows and markets and in print advertising. If people are more interested in "the look" than authenticity, things will change soon.

Preface

To appreciate a hint of the future make sure you understand the three terms noted below.

A table that is described as reclaimed means that the wood used in its construction started its career as a floor or wall in a tiny house in China or Tibet. To reclaim is to recycle lumber, glass, tin, or other architectural leftovers into a new and useful object that carries the patina of 200 years of daily use.

The rugs and tapestries that emerge in random lengths from Asia are often bought as remnants from stalls in village markets. They are then "recycled" into 200 year old seat and couch coverings that are in the forefront of home decoration in the United States.

A "vintage" rug may be 50 to 100 years old and the copies being sold today are direct decendents. "Vintage" refers to the original item. For example, a modern refrigerator made to look like an example from 1930 may be modeled on an original item in the basement.

In the DVD that accompanies this book there is a detailed look at an "American" pie safe that began life in China as a packing crate. The crate, from about 1870, has been reclaimed into an American pie safe. Your grandchildren may treasure it and pass it down as a family heirloom. Keep in mind that it has been closer to the Great Wall than the Oregon Trail.

R.C. Raycraft
Fall 2005

Introduction

"What is Americana?"

We all seem to innately know what Americana is but some of us aren't sure what it isn't. For our purposes "Americana" generates a vivid flashback to a Fourth of July parade in our postcardesque hometown watching from a prime seat on our father's shoulders Cub Scout floats, high school bands, and bemedaled veterans of wars fought before we were born.

It could be Harry Truman, Ike, peanut butter and grape jelly on white bread, Sunday morning doughnuts and the Tribune, falling leaves and football, John Wayne on a Saturday afternoon at the Castle, or the toys of our childhood showing up fifty years later at a flea market and rekindling a flame that we thought was eternally extinguished.

Thomas Wolfe wrote about the difficulty of going home. The trick is to take some home with you wherever the meandering path drops you off. He said you can't go home. If the suitcase is stuffed with some values, three or four family legends, and a quilt, you can.

Are certain categories of Americana more prevelant in one part of the country than another?

Introduction

Twenty years ago there was a significant amount of regional influence in what collectors had the opportunity to purchase. The national influence of the home decorating magazines has rearranged our tastes as consumers. Corn dryers from Illinois, tobacco baskets from Kentucky, watering cans from Ace Hardware on the corner, shabby chic tables from the city dump, and table cloths from Aunt Harriet's estate sale decorate the covers of the monthly publications. Walls of metal lunch boxes from 1950s and 1960s television programs compete with flea market finds for attention. Somebody said "It's not good or bad, it's just different."

Our experience has been that what was "really good" thirty years ago is "great" today and what what was "mediocre" in 1970 is closer to "really good" in 2006. The junk of yesterday that was repainted, reworked, and recycled is still junk even though it might have come in a container from China or be featured on the cover of a magazine.

Where can Americana be found?

If you are in New Hampshire during Antique Week in early August each year and your pockets are extremely deep, you can fill two trucks and own a collection of nineteenth century Americana. There will probably be no bargains but you can be reasonably certain that your merchandise is accurately described by the seller.

If you want eighteenth century American furnishings, it's going to be considerably more difficult and your deep pockets are going to need extensions. You also are going to need some advice and a paddle for the auction. There will be no bargains.

If you want bargains, the key is to find a seller who doesn't know what he/she has for sale. To be successful you are going to have to possess the ability to see and recognize something in a situation where it shouldn't be found. It doesn't take significant knowledge to buy an exceptional example at an upscale antique show. It takes the ability to write the check. The dealers in that environment usually know what they have and price it accordingly.

The dealer who purchases the contents of a house where members of the same family have lived for a century can't be expected to be aware of the value of jewelry, art pottery, military memorabilia, postcards, furniture, paintings, prints, rugs, toys, dishes, and quilts. Hidden within a basement, out building, garage, three floors, and an attic are some semi-treasures. Some of it is going to be overpriced and some is going to be bargain priced. Seldom is something offered for its actual fair market value (assuming there is such a thing).

What is the primary purpose of this book?

The obvious purpose is to enlighten and entertain the reader. If you pick this volume up, put it down, and repeatedly consult it, our mission has been accomplished. There is a wide range of information inside that crosses a multitude of collectible categories.

The DVD

The attached DVD is a primary source of information for collectors of antiques and collectibles because the individuals being interviewed make a living finding, pricing, researching, and offering for sale the items discussed. They understand the price structure of the category and the eccentricities of what makes something "good," "great," and "not so great."

The interviews were conducted at the 3rd Sunday Market in Bloomington, Illinois. There was no script and the discussions were filmed in "real time" as they took place.

The dealers were chosen because they are articulate, informed, and enthusiastic about their offerings. They have something to share with the viewer.

A generation ago there were a multitude of "general line" dealers who offered everything from Depression glass to dry sinks and postcards to pie safes. They found their merchandise when their door bell rang or at the estate sale of the "neighbor lady" across the street. It was a relatively simple operation because most reproductions, fakes, and containers from China were still lingering on the horizon. The business was less intense and certainly not as competitive as it is today.

Information is a very serious commodity. This DVD is designed to offer you a new perspective on buying antiques and collectibles. The probability of a smile is also reasonably high.

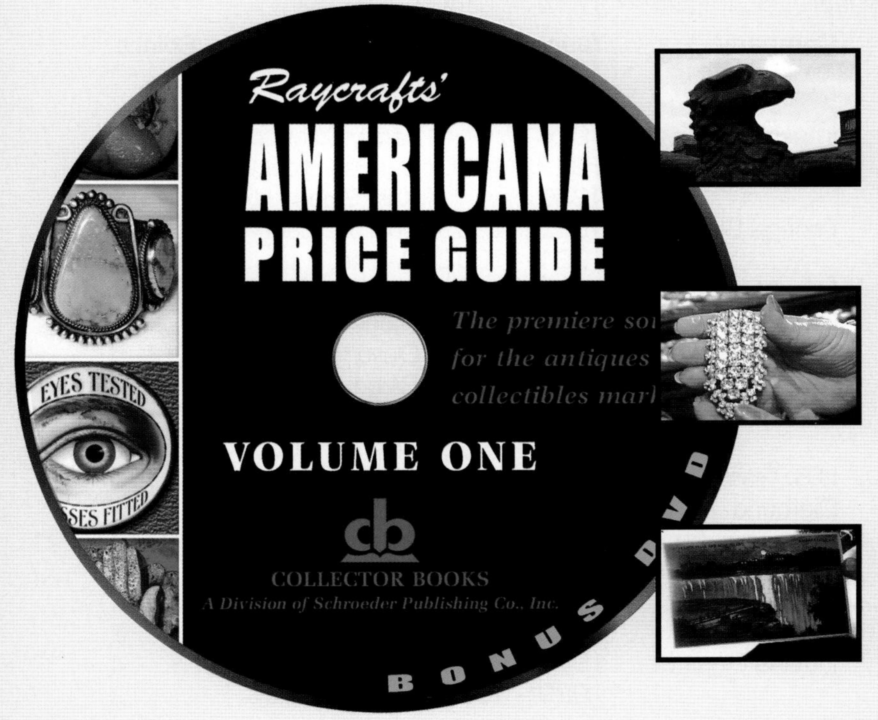

Dates and Chronology

If you are going to collect some aspect of Americana, it is important that you have a cursory knowledge of approximately when a particular item or individual was popular or first came to be manufactured.

The list that follows should provide a basic background that will get the conversation started.

Antique — 100 years old

Art Deco — 1925 – 1940s

Art Nouveau — "new art," 1890s – 1930s

Arts & Crafts — 1890s – early 1920s

Avon Company Inc. — started in 1929

Bakelite — plastic used in handles, radio cases, jewelry, 1900 – 1940s

Barbie® doll — first produced in 1959

Belter furniture — 1880s – 1890s

Cambridge glass — 1901 – 1938

Coca-Cola — 1886

Cracker Jack — packaged with prizes since 1912, after 1948, all plastic

Depression glass — 1914 – 1940

Company	Year	Pattern	Colors
Imperial Glass Co.	1914	Fancy Colonial	6
	1927 – 1930	Beaded Block	7
	1930	Katy Blue	2
Federal Glass Co.	1935 – 1939	Sharon "Cabbage Rose"	4
	1931 – 1932	Parrot	3
Hazel-Atlas Glass Co.	1934	Moderntone	2
	1930 – 1936	Cloverleaf	4
	1930 – 1931	Ribbon	3
	1930	Fruits	3
	1920 – 1926	Colonial Block	3
U.S. Glass Co.	1920s	Aunt Polly	3
Diamond Glassware Co.	1925	Adam's Rib	7
Hocking Glass Co.	1931 – 1935	Princess	4
	1929 – 1933	Black Optic	4
	1928 – 1930	Spiral	2
Indiana Glass Co.	1926 – 1931	Tea Room	4
	1929 – 1932	Lorain "Basket"	3

Company	Year	Pattern	Colors
Jeannette Glass Co.	1928 – 1932	Iris	2
	1929 – 1930	Cube "Cubist"	3
	1930	Cherry Blossom	4
	1931 – 1933	Sierra	2
	1932 – 1934	Adam	5
	1930 – 1934	Sunflower	3
MacBeth-Evans Glass Co.	1930 – 1936	S Pattern	2
	1930 – 1934	Dogwood	4
	1930 – 1936	American Sweetheart	5

Eastlake — a furniture style of simple design, after Civil War, 1865 to 1880s

Fenton Art Glass — 1905 – 1970, with paper labels

Fiesta dinnerware — 1936 – 1973, Homer Laughlin China Co., West Virginia

The absolute *least* you need to know if you are going to collect

1936 — Fiesta dinnerware first manufactured by Homer Laughlin China Co.

1936 — The original colors were cobalt blue, red, yellow, light green, and ivory.

1937 — Turquoise Fiesta is added to the list of colors.

1950s — Forest green, chartreuse, gray, medium green, and join the list of colors.

1936 — 1969 The only color that was consistently manufactured during this period was yellow.

1969 Fiesta dinnerware is discontinued.

1969 Fiesta Ironstone is introduced.

1986 Fiesta dinnerware is brought back with new colors.

Notes

1. A Fiesta individual teapot in ivory (one of three thought to exist) sold in 2004 for a shade over $20,000.00.
2. From the 1980s sapphire blue and lilac were only offered for a brief period and are very collectible.
3. For vintage Fiesta collectors (1936 – 1969) medium green is the desired color of the moment.
4. Like every other antique or collectible, condition and surface are absolutely essential in determining value.

Fostoria pressed glass — 1887 – 1986, numerous colors and patterns

Gaudy Welsh — English pottery exported to U.S., 1830s – 1860s

gutta-percha — 1850s – 1870s, used to make photographic case often for two pictures, hard rubber substance, imported from Asia

Hall China — East Liverpool, Ohio, made Autumn Leaf dinnerware and teapots, c. 1920

Harlequin — dinnerware from Homer Laughlin China, sold in dimestores, 1938

Hummel — first appeared in 1935 from designs of Berta Hummel (Sister Innocentia), started by F.W. Goebel Company in Germany in 1871

Imperial Glass Corp. (Lenox Inc.) — made Candlewick glass, 1936 – 1982

Victorian — a period of "more is better, much better," 1830s – early 1900s

head vase — an inexpensive vase of a lady from the shoulders up, offered by florists from the 1930s through the 1960s, sold with a bouquet

Heisey glass — 1896 – 1957

Hitchcock chairs — 1820s – 1950s

Homer Laughlin China Company — opened in 1871

Hoosier kitchen cabinets — made in several forms by different companies from c. 1895 to early 1940s

Insulators — from the telegraph and telephone invention, first appeared with the coming of the telegraph after 1850, glass or pottery

James Beam Distilling Company — started making figural (decorative) whiskey decanters in 1955

Jugtown — pottery in North Carolina that opened in 1920

Kentucky Derby glasses — mint julep glasses offered at the event since 1940

Lenox china — White House china since 1917, started in 1906

Lladro — porcelain from Spain since 1951

Madame Alexander dolls — 1923

Marx toys — 1921

matchbook covers — c. 1892

McKinley Tariff Act — March 1, 1891, all items imported into U.S. had to be marked with country of origin

mercury dime — first minted in 1916

Mettlach — German company that made steins, tiles, and vases, closed in 1921

Mission — furniture style popular after 1895 to about 1915

Monmouth (Illinois) Pottery — opened in 1892, variety of stoneware products, sold to Western Stoneware Co. in 1906

Nippon — Between 1891 and 1921 products from Japan were marked "Nippon." After 1921 those goods were labeled "Japan." The country of origin (after 1921) had to be written in English. From 1945 to 1951 the term was "Occupied Japan" for goods from Japan.

pilgrim century — 1600s, seventeenth century

Sandwich Glass — 1825 – 1888 (Boston and Sandwich Glass Co.)

Precious Moments — made since 1979

Roseville — Ohio pottery that produced art pottery, 1890 – 1954

Roycroft — industry formed by Hudson, Illinois, native Elbert Hubbard. Created Arts & Crafts furniture, lighting, art, and a magazine. Hubbard died on the Lusitania in 1915. Company lasted until 1938.

Schoenhut — Philadelphia toy company that offered a huge assortment of dolls, games, circus toys, etc. Early 1900s – mid-1930s. The circus figures, animals, tents, and accessories are perhaps the best remembered.

Stickley furnishings — 1902 – 1923, made Mission furniture and hammered copper decorations for homes, Stickley Furniture Co.

Gustav Stickley — died in 1942, competed with his brothers, L. and J.G., manufactured Mission furniture in oak. Many collectors consider Gustav the "father" of the Mission furniture movement.

Stiegel glass — glassware made in central Pennsylvania in the mid-eighteenth century by Baron Stiegel. Often confused with etched glass made in Europe about the same time.

Louis Comfort Tiffany — died in 1933. Designed lamps and shades in his studio. His father, Charles, who died in 1902, opened the jewelry store.

Steiff — German company that made (makes) stuffed toys. They can be dated as follows:

1948 — 1953, U.S. Zone, Germany, on a cloth tag
1940 — ear button with raised block letters "Steiff"
1950s — ear button with raised letters in script
late 1960s — letters incised (impressed into) the ear button

Watt Pottery — hand-decorated pottery popular from 1930s to 1965, opened in 1922 in Ohio, purchased Globe Pottery in early 1920s

Winchester 1873 rifle — 1873 – 1919, 15 shots, numerous styles and woods

Zanesville Pottery — 1900 – 1962, Zanesville, Ohio

Prices

How to Read a Price Tag

Dealers who set up at antiques shows, markets, or the parking lots of the local American Legion on every other Sunday morning are in attendance to *sell* their merchandise. Most items for sale have a price tag or sticker. The dealers all have costs to cover in doing business. They have booth or table rental for space. There are fees for electricity, motels and hotels, gas, insurance, food, porters, and walls or backdrops in some situations. In an urban setting there are numerous other fees and parking costs that have to be absorbed.

All of the above enter into the price of the piece you want to purchase. The critical piece of information to memorize is that the exhibitor/dealer would not be there if he/she/they did not want, to varying degrees, to sell their merchandise.

To assist you in deciphering the asking price as illustrated on the tag or sticker, we offer the following insights. We have included four examples of the same copper wash boiler on a price tag.

A. Factory-made American wash boiler, missing lid, c. 1900, $125, D.105
B. Factory-made American wash boiler, missing lid, c. 1900, $125 net.
C. Factory-made American wash boiler, missing lid, c. 1900, $125 0346-501
D. Factory-made American wash boiler, missing lid, c. 1900, $125 bek se

In the first example the seller will offer the boiler to a "dealer" for $105. Typically, anyone who asks for a better price "dealer" or not can make a purchase for $105.

"Net" indicates that the seller is not willing to deduct anything from the price. This can often be because that is the approximate amount the seller has invested in the piece.

The 0346 is the inventory number of the boiler. The 501 is the selling price backwards.

"BEK" translates into $105.

The letters "se" inform the seller that the original cost of the boiler was $60. A sale at $105 would provide a profit of $45 before prorated expenses are considered.

B L A C K S T O N E
1 2 3 4 5 6 7 8 9 0

The obvious problem happens when a 10-letter word other than BLACKSTONE is selected by the seller as the code word.

The word CHARLESTON is also commonly used by many dealers and retail shop owners.

Clocks

Gem Razor, 1910 – 1920, $1,200.00.

Mercury Outboard Motors Sales & Service, lighted top, works, $375.00.

Flying A, metal with metal toy truck with neon surrounding the truck, 24" x 25" x 6", $900.00.

Royal Crown, 1940s, $350.00.

Coca-Cola, 1950s, "fish-tail" design, $300.00.

A C Spark plugs, 1960s, plastic, $250.00.

Coca-Cola, 1950s small, $300.00.

Grapette, 1950s, $300.00.

Orange Crush, 1960s, $200.00.

Squirt, 1970s, square, $200.00.

Hires Root Beer, 1950s, $350.00.

Nu-Grape, 1950s, $350.00.

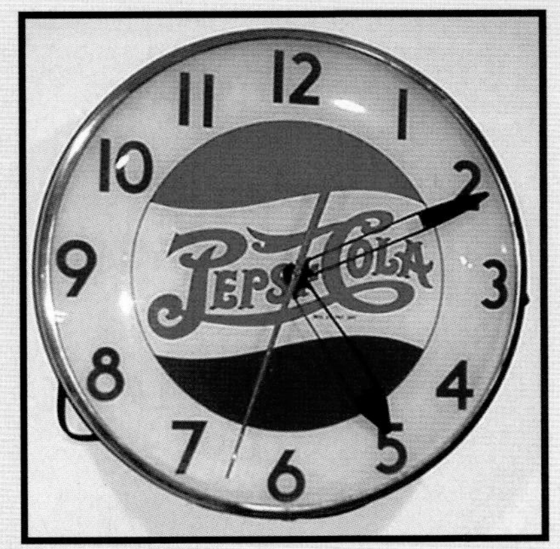

Pepsi-Cola, single dot, $300.00.

Coca-Cola, 1950s, with bottle, $400.00.

Pepsi-Cola, 1960s, bottle cap, $300.00.

Pepsi, 1970s, "Say Pepsi Please," $285.00.

Faultless Feeds, 1950s, double bubble, $200.00.

Hires Root Beer, 1950s, $350.00.

Chevrolet, neon, 21" x 6", good condition, from Johnson Chevrolet (Indianapolis), $950.00.

Fisk Tires, neon spinner with tire, 30" x 9", very good condition, $9,500.00.

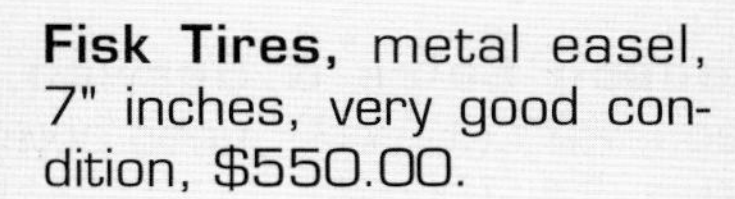
Fisk Tires, metal easel, 7" inches, very good condition, $550.00.

MoPar Parts & Accessories, neon, 16", works great, $1,900.00.

GMC Trucks Sales & Service, neon, 19" x 19" x 7", good condition, $1,900.00.

Hudson Sales & Service, neon, 22" x 6" x 7", good condition, $1,700.00.

Automobile Related Signs

Mother Penn Motor Oil, die cut, 20" x 30",with Ma Penn, good gloss, $1,300.00.

Mother Penn Motor Oil, die cut 6" x 9",with Ma Penn, good gloss, $350.00.

Globe Gasoline, 42", $4,500.00.

Globe Gasoline, 42", $800.00.

Marathon Ethyl, 30", $700.00.

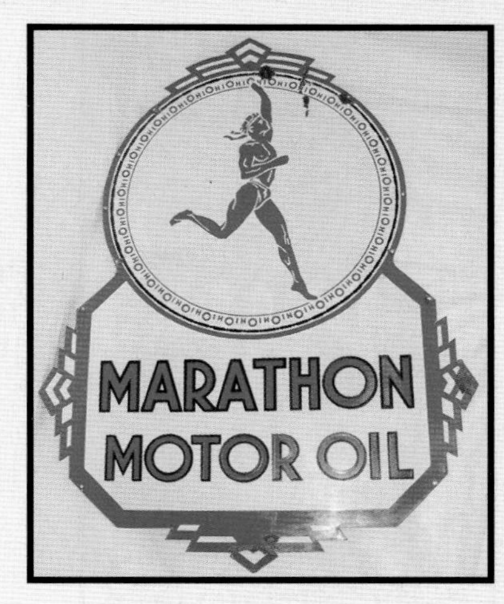

Marathon Motor Oil, die cut porcelain, 57" x 42", $3,750.00.

Marathon Products, 48", $5,250.00.

Marathon, 24" x 36", $125.00.

Pearl Oil Kerosene, tin flange, 19" x 12", dated 1947, $1,400.00.

Socony No. 1 Aircraft Oil, lubster, 9½" x 8", $850.00.

Mobil Pegasus, die cut, 72" x 96", excellent gloss, $3,400.00.

Socony Motor Gasoline, porcelain flange, 24" x 20", $1,900.00.

Universal Batteries, 48" x 12", $1,900.00.

Universal Batteries, die cut, 20" x 20", $1,200.00.

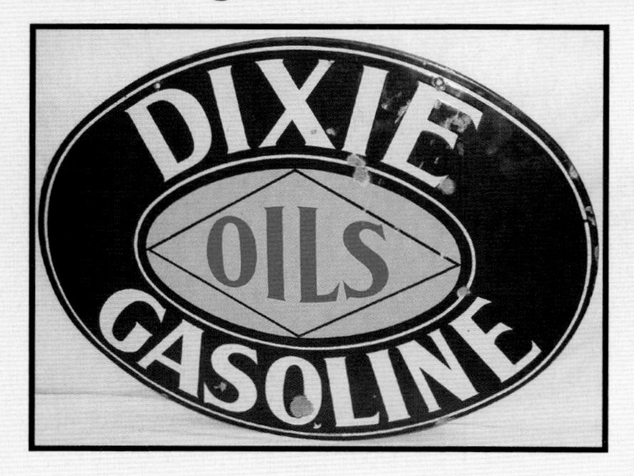

Dixie Oils & Gasoline,
20" x 30", $750.00.

Associated Gasoline,
27½", $475.00.

Power Lube Motor Oil,
20" x 28", $600.00.

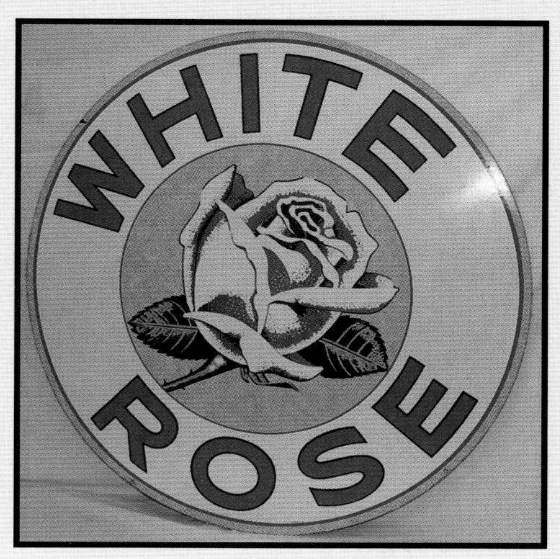

White Rose, 36", dated 1946, $2,750.00.

Motor Oil, self framed, 16" x 95", $450.00.

Gasoline, self framed, 16" x 95", good gloss, $550.00.

White Rose, with side brackets, 18" x 18", $125.00.

White Rose, with side brackets, 18" x 18", $100.00.

Note the slight condition differences that make a $25.00 price difference in the two White Rose signs.

Union Gasoline, die cut, 32" x 26", $350.00.

Havoline Motor Oil, porcelain flange, 20" x 12", $400.00.

Sinclair Opaline Motor Oil, 24", $1,200.00.

Sunray Oils, octagon, 25", $1,000.00.

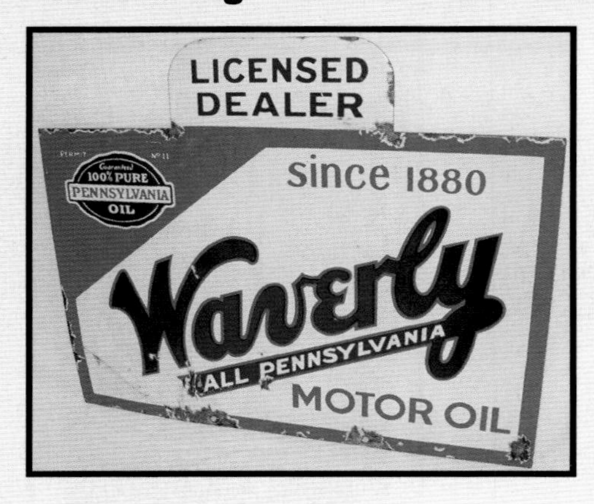

Waverly Motor Oil, die cut, 20" x 24", $200.00.

Penn Drake Motor Oil, embossed, 10" x 28", with logo, $375.00.

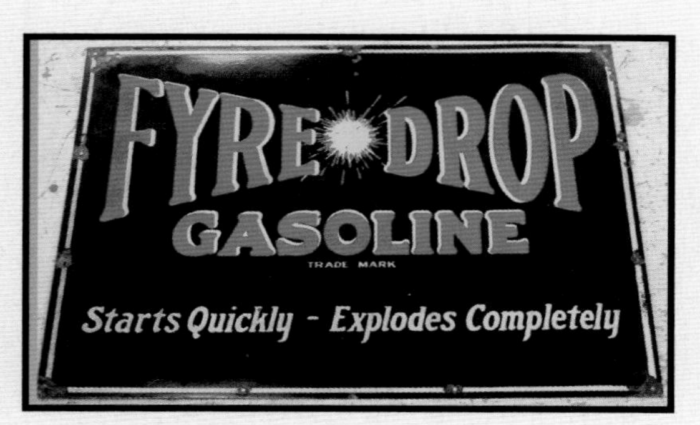

Fire Drop Gasoline, 28" x 40", $1,400.00.

Wm. Penn Motor Oils, porcelain die cut flange, 16" x 18", $450.00.

Dixie Oils & Gasoline, "The Power to Pass, That's Dixie Gas," wood back, 48" x 72", $900.00.

Texaco Marine Lubricants, 15" x 30", dated 1947, $1,500.00.

Atlantic Motor Oil, wooden framed, 44" x 14", $1,500.00.

Sinclair Opaline Motor Oil, 60" x 15", $350.00.

Hudson, cardboard poster, 37" x 23", $550.00.

Coop Gasoline Motor Oil, 40", good gloss, $2,000.00.

Socony Motor Oil, porcelain flange, 24" x 20", $350.00.

Sinclair Opaline Motor Oil, 28" x 72", $750.00.

Mobiloil, keyhole with bracket, 32" x 36", $700.00.

Standard Oil Zerolene, truck door, 6", $2,800.00.

Sinclair Opaline Motor Oil, lubster, $0.00.

Time Super Gasoline, 14" x 9", $800.00.

Signal Ethyl Gasoline, 12", $900.00.

Texaco Motor Oil, porcelain flange, 23" x 18", $800.00.

Refiners Gasoline & Motor Oils, 36", $1,800.00.

Federal Extra Service, mounted in original wood frame, 19" x 38", $2,100.00.

Polarine Motor Oil, 28" x 60", $900.00.

Texaco Motor Oil, porcelain flange, 23" x 18", $800.00.

Husky Service, shield shaped, 48" x 42", $17,500.00.

Husky Gasoline, 42", $5,000.00.

Husky 1 Mile, metal die cut, 24" x 21", $750.00.

Mobiloil Race Engines, die cut, 9" x 16", $12,500.00.

Mobiloil D, 9" x 11", $1,400.00.

Conoco Motor Oil, porcelain flange, 19" x 20", $7,500.00.

Conoco Gasoline, 26", $2,500.00.

Conoco Gasoline, 14" x 14", $900.00.

Goodrich Safety Tires, wood framed, 63" x 18", $6,000.00.

Good Year Tires, die cut, 15" x 26", very good gloss, $2,100.00.

Good Year Tires, porcelain die cut flange, 34" x 22", $600.00.

Kelly Tires, tin flange, 24" x 24", $4,500.00.

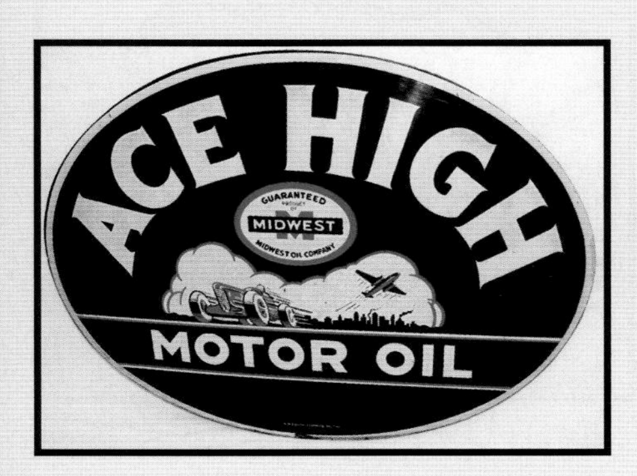

Ace High Motor Oil, 18 x 23", dated 1941, $4,750.00.

Skylark Aviation Grade Gasoline, neon with can, 42" x 66", $9,000.00.

United Motors Service, neon, 21" x 36", $2,000.00.

Smith's Savings Service, neon, 70" x 70", $2,250.00.

Associated Flying A, tin neon, 10" x 19", $350.00.

Phillips 66, neon with can, 30" x 30", $2,700.00.

Hi-Speed, die cut neon, 42" x 100", $3,750.00.

Alemite Genuine Lubrication Service, die cut neon with can, 96" x 24", $2,500.00.

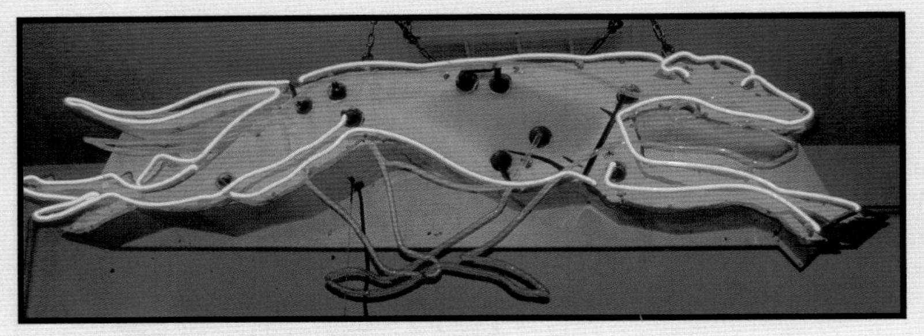

Running Greyhound Bus, die cut neon with can, 22" x 84", $4,750.00.

Shell, embossed neon, 48" x 48", $1,400.00.

Richlube Motor Oil, 24", $4,500.00.

Richfield Ethyl, 25", $4,250.00.

Texas Pacific Gasoline & Motor Oil, 42", $2,750.00.

Lanes Gasoline, 30", fantasy sign, $700.00.

Velco Motor Oil, tombstone, 30" x 20", $700.00.

Navy Gasoline, 30", $3,250.00.

Hood Tires, die cut, 71" x 22", $7,500.00.

Hood Tires, 78" x 18", $1,000.00.

Hood Tires, die cut, 35" x 12", $400.00.

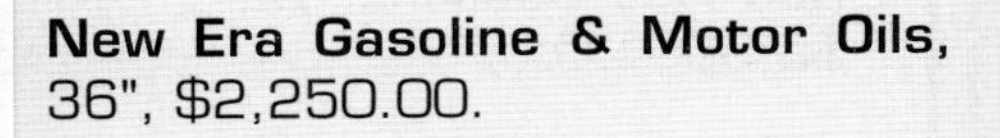

New Era Gasoline & Motor Oils, 36", $2,250.00.

Wings Motor Oil, tombstone, 35" x 26", $550.00.

Red Hat Motor Oil, 32", $8,500.00.

Red Hat Gasoline, 32", $2,500.00.

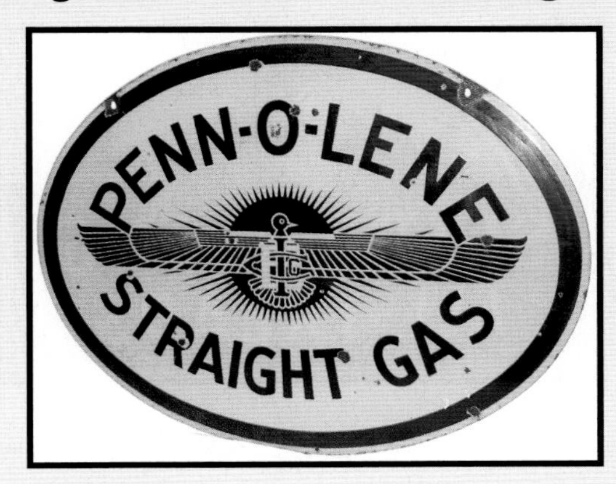

Penn-O-Lene, 36" x 48", $2,100.00.

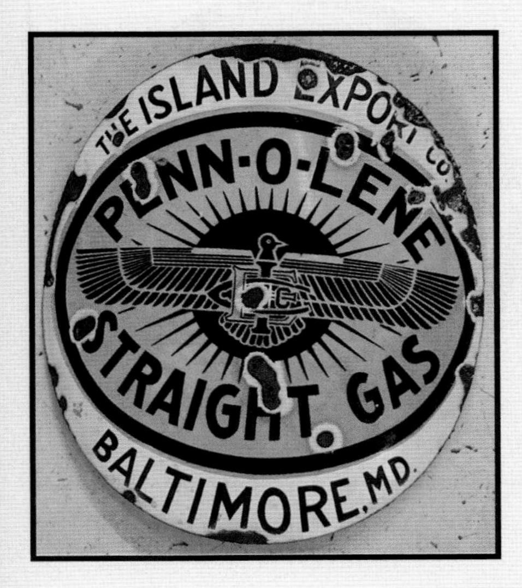

Penn-O-Lene, curved, 12" x 11", $300.00.

Panhandle, 50" x 69", $4,000.00.

Seiberling All-Treads, with milk glass letters, 44" x 70", $2,750.00.

Johnson Motor Oil, "Time tells," $8,000.00.

Johnson Winged 70 Gasolene, tombstone, 36" x 24", $6,500.00.

Marine Gasoline, 58" x 30", $5,750.00.

Globe Battery Station, 20", $450.00.

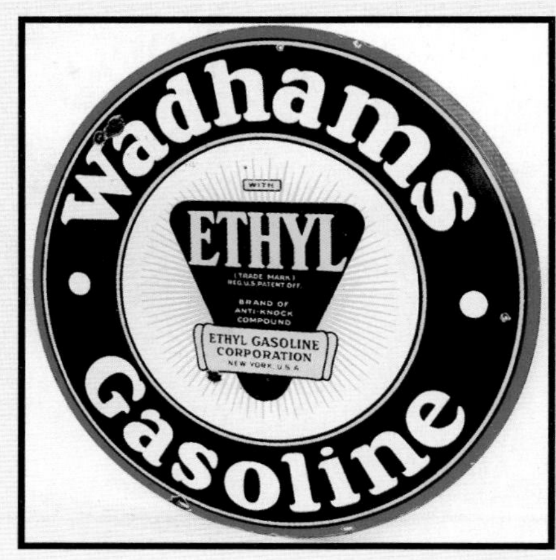

Wadhams Gasoline, 30", $1,300.00.

Pontiac, neon sign with can, 46" x 66", $5,800.00.

Pontiac Authorized Service, 42", $2,750.00.

Pontiac Approved Accessories, masonite die cut, 12" x 13", $1,000.00.

Cadillac V-8, V-16 LaSalle V-8, 24" x 30", $10,000.00.

OK Used Cars, bull nose, 39" x 60", $4,250.00.

GMC Gasoline Diesel Trucks, reverse painted back lit spinner display, 18" x 6", good condition, $1,800.00.

Buick Authorized Service, neon with can, 42", $5,250.00.

Buick Authorized Service, 42", $2,000.00.

Buick Authorized Service, 42", $900.00.

Buick Hall Motor Co., 14" x 19", $475.00.

Willys Overland, neon with can, 34" x 70", $3,000.00.

Willys Jeep Sales & Service, 30" x 48", $4,000.00.

Willys Knight Genuine Service Parts, 30" x 40', $1,300.00.

Overland Motor Cars, porcelain flange sign, 16" x 26", $4,250.00.

Whippet Willys-Overland, 10" x 21", $425.00.

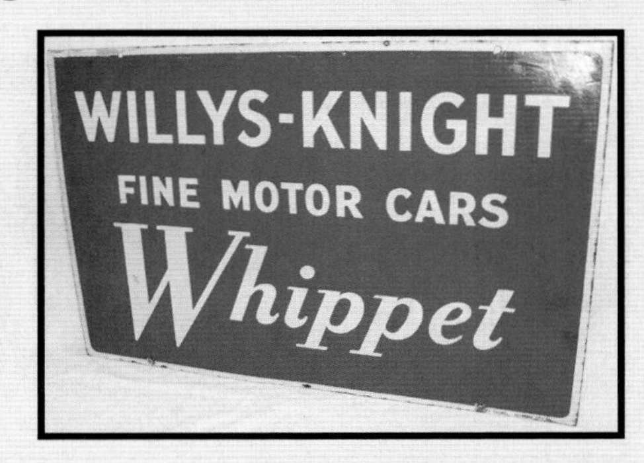

Willys - Knight Whippet, 24" x 36", $650.00.

Chrysler Marine Engine Service, 42", $4,000.00.

Dodge Dependable Service, 42", $2,500.00.

Desoto Plymouth, die cut neon with can, 30" x 62", $1,900.00.

Chrysler Plymouth Approved Service, die cut, 42" x 44", very good gloss, $3,000.00.

Plymouth Chrysler Service, 22" x 18", $2,750.00.

Desoto Plymouth Sales & Service, self framed, $6,750.00.

Dodge Trucks Sales & Service, 42" x 42", very good gloss, nice sign, $6,500.00.

Desoto Plymouth Approved Service, two-piece, 60", $2,000.00.

Magnolene Ford Oil, porcelain flange, 16" x 22", $1,800.00.

Brown's - Oyl For Fords, 20" x 13", $900.00.

Durant Motor Cars, 28" x 42", $3,250.00.

Dort Motor Cars, wood framed, 48" x 95", $1,000.00.

Duesenberg Straight 8, 28" x 72", $700.00.

Chrysler Service, die cut, 21" x 28", $1,700.00.

Studebaker Service Station, 14" x 30", $550.00.

Packard Genuine Service Parts, triangle, 30" x 30", $4,000.00.

Packard Service, die cut with hanging bracket, 42" x 27", $6,500.00.

Willys-Overland Touch-Up Paints, metal display rack with cardboard sign and paint jars, 17" x 25" x 10", $600.00.

30-Willys Overland one ounce touch paint jars and original box.

Chrysler Plymouth Sales & Services, $2,900.00.

Plymouth, wooden and metal die cut, 32" x 100", $850.00.

GMC Gasoline Diesel Trucks, 30", $1,600.00.

Oldsmobile Service, 18" x 36", $350.00.

Studebaker Authorized Service Parts, masonite die cut, 9" x 13", $525.00.

Ford 1957 Ford Galigher Motor Sales, reflector zed, 12" x 38", $325.00.

Studebaker Cars • Trucks, 18", $225.00.

GM Hydra-Matic Drive, die cut, 20" x 24", $2,600.00.

Nash Authorized Service die cut, 36" x 22", $3,000.00.

Dodge Save Six Barrel Of Gas, masonite and wood easel, 39" x 27", $1,250.00.

Maxwell Service, 24" x 24", has been restored, $1,300.00.

GMC Trucks Sales & Service, 42", $2,300.00.

Ford Lincoln Fordson Cars Trucks Tractors, 27" x 65", $1,800.00.

Studebaker Authorized Service, 48", $700.00.

Chevrolet Genuine Parts, die cut sign, 19" x 24", $3,500.00.

Ford Authorized Service Station, 27" x 60", $900.00.

Oakland Pontiac Sales & Service, 24" x 36", $1,300.00.

Chevrolet Sales & Service, 28" x 40", good gloss, $1,200.00.

Nash Bonded Used Cars, 42", $3,700.00.

Rambler Nash Hudson Parts & Service, die cut, 36" x 42", $4,600.00.

Nash Service Parts, die cut, 46" x 46" $700.00.

Oldsmobile, 20", $1,800.00.

Star Cars Authorized Service, 24" x 36", $1,100.00.

Kaiser Frazer Approved Service, 60", $1,300.00.

Hudson Parts & Service, die cut, 30" x 42", $1,200.00.

Crosley Sales & Service, 42", $2,400.00.

Rambler Parts & Service, 42", $1,100.00.

Oldsmobile Service, 42", $750.00.

Minneapolis - Moline Sales & Service, neon with can, 46" x 66", $4,500.00.

International Harvester, neon sign with can, 52" x 46", $2,000.00.

Gleaner Baldwin Combines, neon with can, 27" x 40", $1,500.00.

Case Sales & Service, tin flange, 33" x 22", $1,100.00.

Caterpillar Farm Tractors, 24" x 72", $3,000.00.

Continental Station Service, 16" x 20", $2,200.00.

Ferguson System, 11" x 22", $450.00.

McCormick Deering Machines, embossed, 12" x 16", $350.00.

Gleaner Baldwin Cabins, porcelain flange, 18" x 20", $350.00.

John Deere Farm Implements, 24" x 72", $2,250.00.

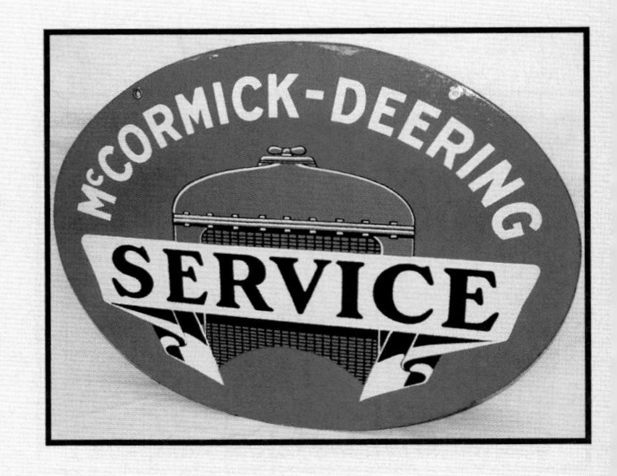

McCormick Deering, 24" x 32", $2,750.00.

Desoto Service, 22" x 18", $5,000.00.

Hupmobile Service, 16" x 30", $450.00.

Oliver Tractor Implements, tin flange, 18" x 18", $900.00.

Rauscher's Service Stations, 60" x 36", $800.00.

Chevrolet Genuine Part, tin flange, 18" x 19", $600.00.

Colonial Lubrication Service, 30" x 30", $2,000.00.

Thomas Glass Sales & Service, die cut, 22" x 30", $2,000.00.

Liberty Gasoline, 48" x 30", $4,250.00.

OK (Chevrolet used cars), 30", $1,000.00.

Case Farm Machinery, embossed, 30" x 72", $650.00.

Red Indian Motor Oils, self-framed, 24" x 17", $4,000.00.

Snow Bird Motor Oil, embossed, 30" x 22", $900.00.

David Brown Tractors & Implements, 30" x 18", $650.00.

Colonial, 72" x 66", $600.00.

New Idea Farm Equipment, 18" x 40", $2,100.00.

Sinclair Aircraft, with bracket, 48", $3,000.00.

Imperial Refineries, 30", $1,500.00.

Bell Gasoline, 40", $700.00.

Bell Gasoline & Oils, die cut, 48" x 48", $400.00.

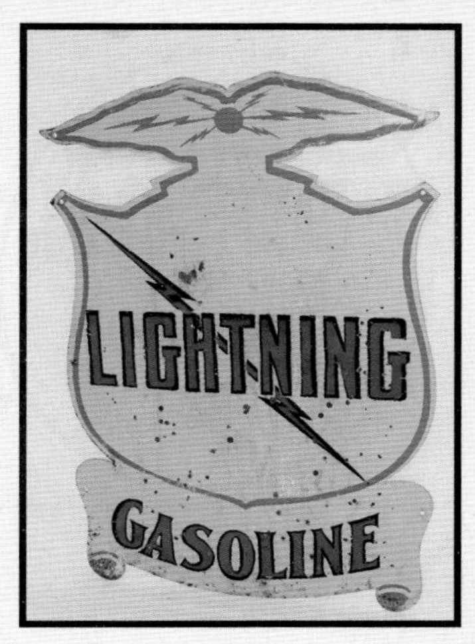

Lightning Gasoline, die cut, 28" x 18", $650.00.

Magnolia Gasoline, 30", $1,600.00.

Magnolia Magnolene Motor Oils, 30", $400.00.

Hudson Built Car Authorized Service, 36", $1,000.00.

Atlantic Gasoline, 52" x 36", $400.00.

Raleigh, die cut, mounted on wood, 48" x 39", hand on woman has been replaced, $13,000.00.

Whizzer Authorized Sales & Service, metal and glass reverse painted back lit counter display, 7" x 19" x 6", $425.00.

Mercury Outboards, die cut neon with can, 21" x 38", $1,600.00.

Johnson Outboard Motors, metal and glass reverse painted back lit counter display, 12" x 25" x 5", $450.00.

Lubri-Gas Homogenized Fuel, 19" x 28", $275.00.

Sea Sled Boats, 15" x 28", $350.00.

Vacuum Marine Motor Oil, embossed sign, 10" x 28", $1,100.00.

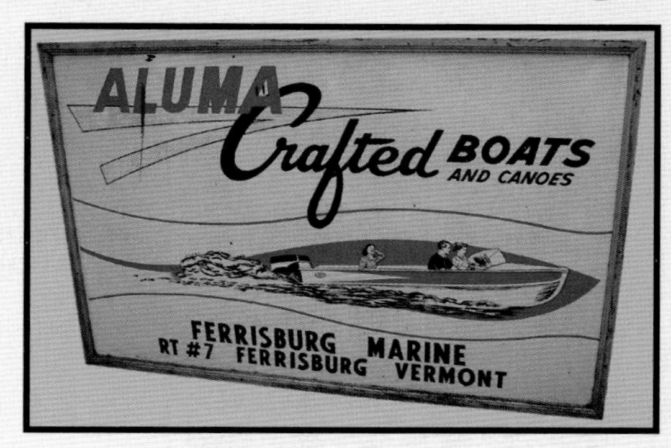

Aluma Crafted Boats, wood framed, 48" x 72", $650.00.

Harley Davidson Oil, 9" x 14", $1,500.00.

Hopper's Cycles, die cut, 18" x 15", $350.00.

Mercury Outboards, embossed sign, 30" x 30", $375.00.

OMC Snow Cruiser, $500.00.

Rudge Whitworth Coventry Cycles, porcelain die cut flange, 12" x 25", $600.00.

Great Western Gasoline Engine, 9" x 20", $90.00.

Empire Red Chief Implements, 8" x 24", $375.00.

Hudson Essex Service, 16" x 30", $1,000.00.

GE Appliances, neon with can, 42" x 64", $1,000.00.

Auto-Lite Electric Service, die cut neon with can, 34" x 54", $1,600.00.

Red Goose Shoes, diecut neon with neon tubes, 50" x 49", $2,000.00.

Red Goose Shoes, die cut, 60" x 42", $700.00.

Blue Seal Motor Oil, 30", $375.00.

GAS, neon, 26", $1,300.00.

Morris Trucks, die cut, 22" x 16", $5,300.00.

Lister Diesel, 29" x 19", $1,000.00.

REO Sales Service, tombstone, 30" x 20", $1,800.00.

Chalmers Service, 20" x 30", $1,800.00.

Fargo Approved Service, 30", $2,200.00.

Fargo Trucks two bull nosed signs mounted together, 9" x 59" x 6", $800.00.

Federal Trucks Sales & Service, 18" x 30", $1,400.00.

International Trucks, 24" x 45", $2,300.00.

Fiat Service, self framed, 31" x 40", $700.00.

Republic Authorized Service, 27" x 48", $2,500.00.

Saab Service, convex, 19" x 16", $300.00.

Cushman Motor Scooters, 9" x 12", $250.00.

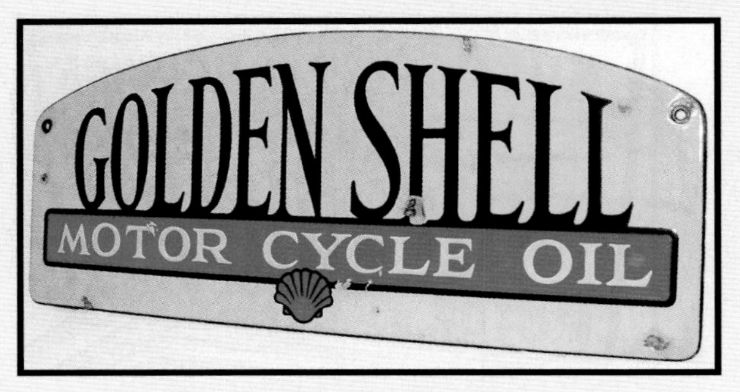

Golden Shell Motor Cycle Oil, 9" x 22", $750.00.

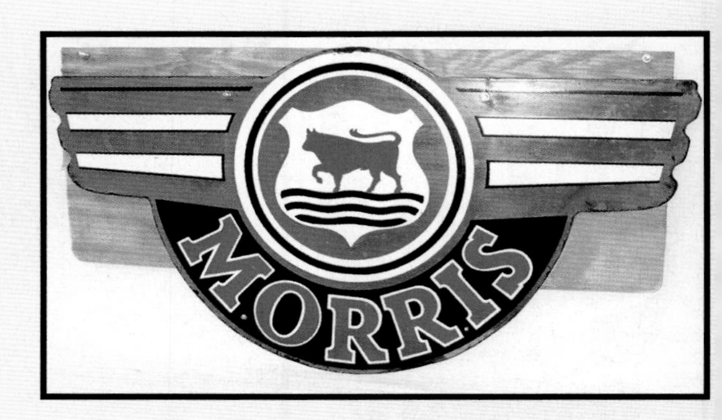

Morris Trucks, die cut mounted on wood, 15" x 29", $600.00.

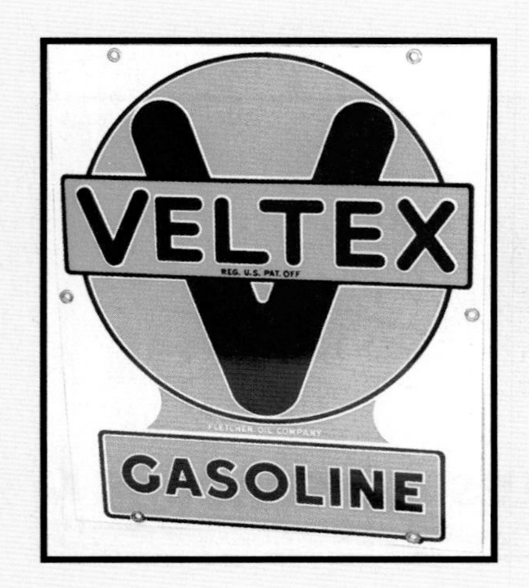

Veltex Gasoline, 15" x 12", $1,200.00.

Wright Aircraft Engines, 10" x 10", $425.00.

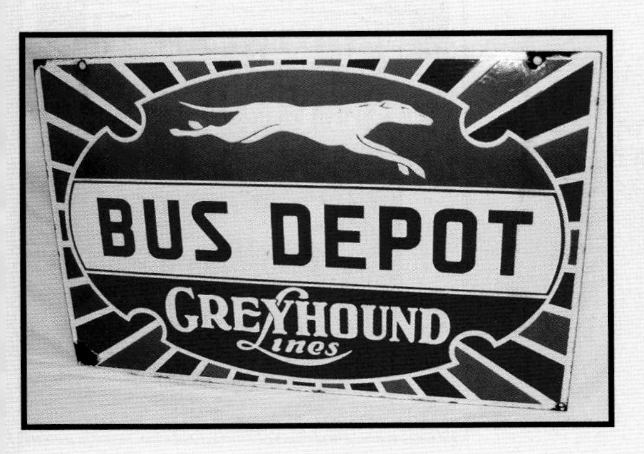

Greyhound Lines Bus Depot, 20" x 30", $1,600.00.

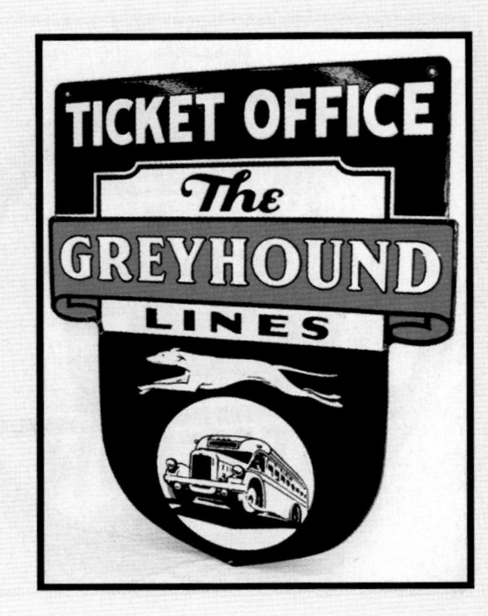

Greyhound Lines, die cut, 31" x 25", $9,500.00.

Northland Greyhound Bus Depot, die cut, 20" x 30", $4,750.00.

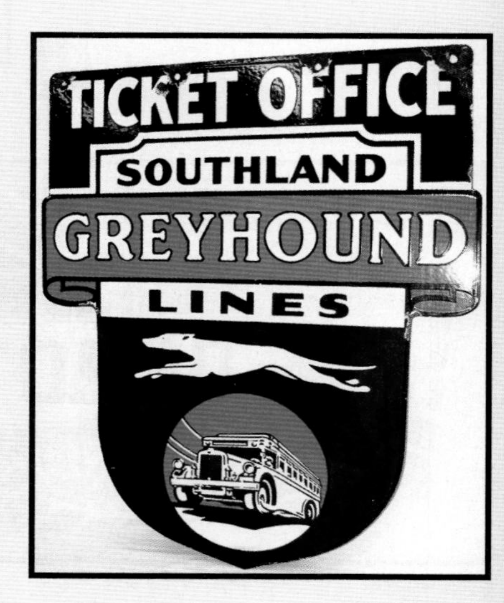

Greyhound Lines Bus Depot, die cut, 30" x 25", $4,000.00.

Bus Station, 16", $750.00.

Black & White Motorway, die cut, 36" x 15" (United Kingdom), $2,100.00.

Associated Motorways Booking Office, tin flange, 12" x 18", $1,000.00.

Peter Pan Bus Lines, die cut, 15" x 22", $375.00.

Silver Eagle, die cut bus emblem, 18" x 38", $75.00.

American Airlines, 21" x 11", $1,400.00.

Gray Coach Lines, two-piece with hanging bracket, 39" x 27", $1,300.00.

Greyhound Line, 20" x 28", $350.00.

Bus Stop D.C. Transit, cast metal, $25.00.

Illinois Farm Supply Gasoline Motor, 42", $400.00.

The information and photos for the sign section were provided by Aumann Auctions. For more information about Aumann Auctions see page 342.

Thermometers

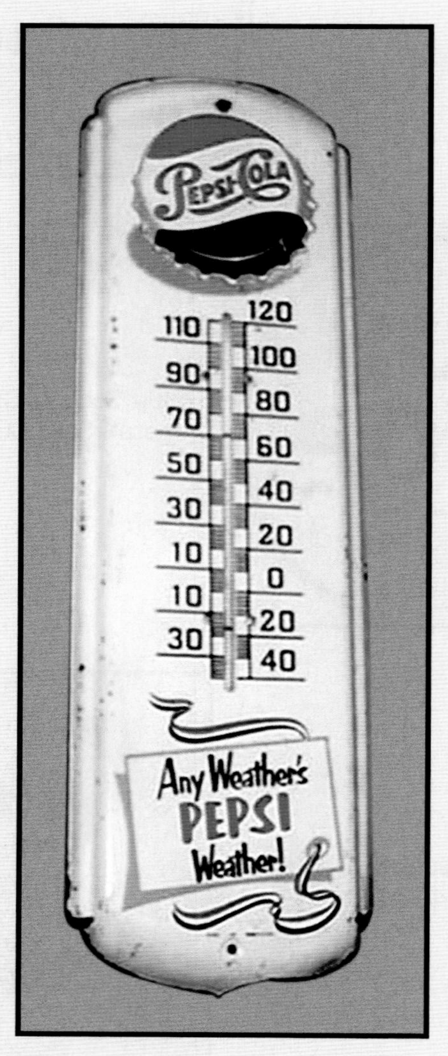

Pepsi-Cola, 1950s, "weather," $300.00.

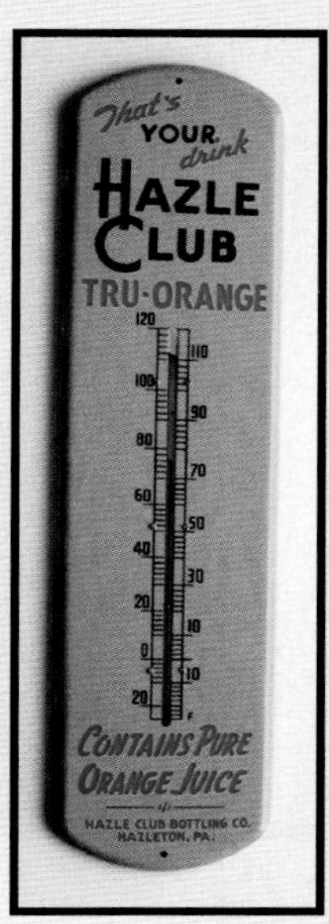

Hazel Club, 1950s, $350.00.

Hicks Gas scale thermometer, 1950s, $400.00.

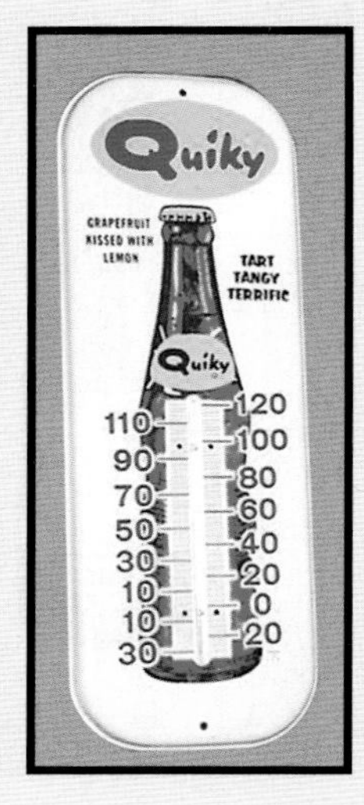

Quiky Pop, 1950s, $150.00.

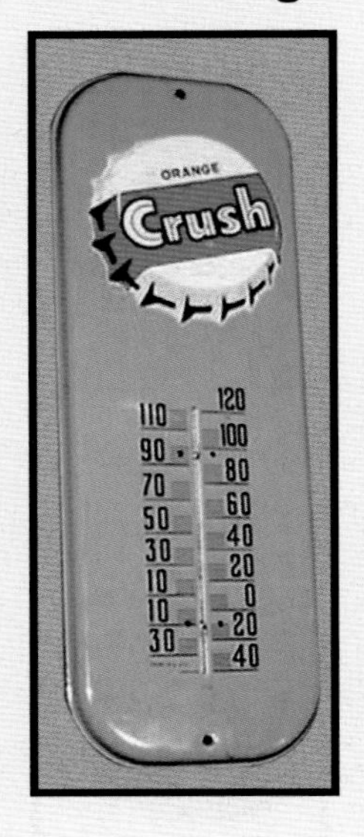

Orange Crush, 1960s, bottle cap, $200.00.

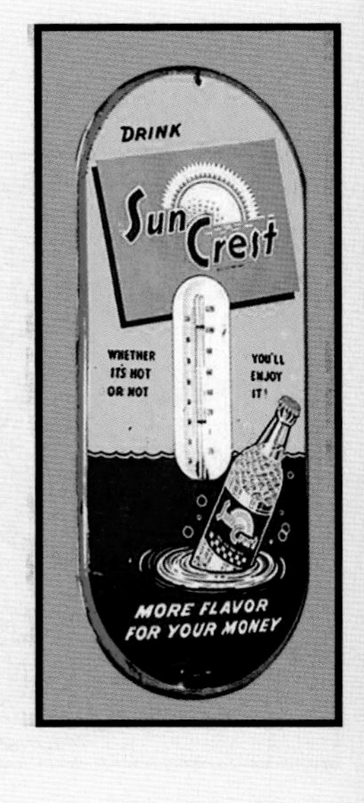

Sun Crest, 1950s, with bottle, $250.00.

7 Up, 1940s, porcelain, $250.00.

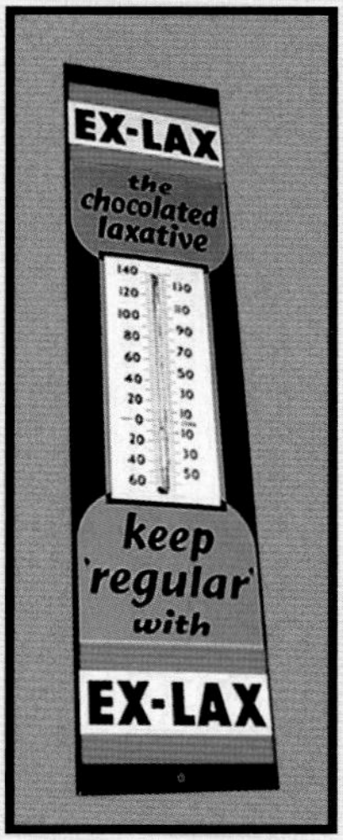

Ex-Lax, 1940s, porcelain, $250.00.

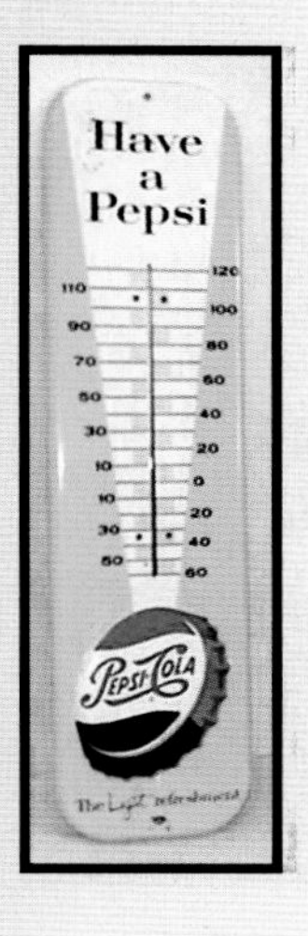

Pepsi, 1960s, bottlecap, $200.00.

Frostie Root Beer, 1960s, $225.00.

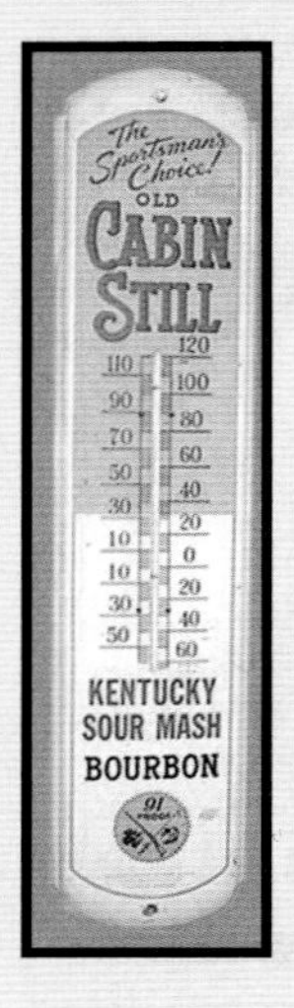

Cabin Still Whiskey, 1960s, $125.00 – 150.00.

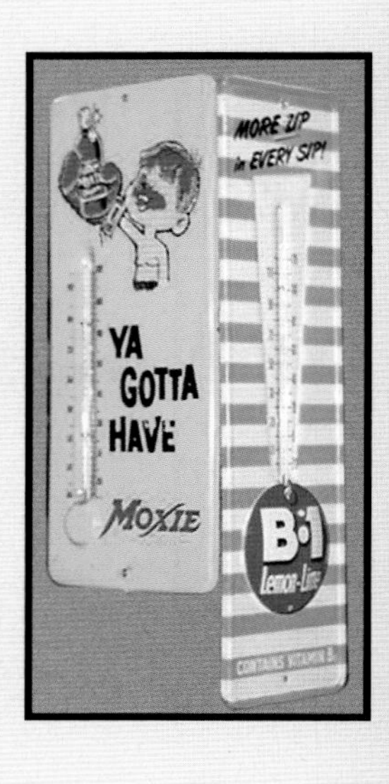

Moxie, 1960s, $250.00.
B I Lemon Lime, $125.00.

Frostie, 1960s, four season favorite, $250.00.

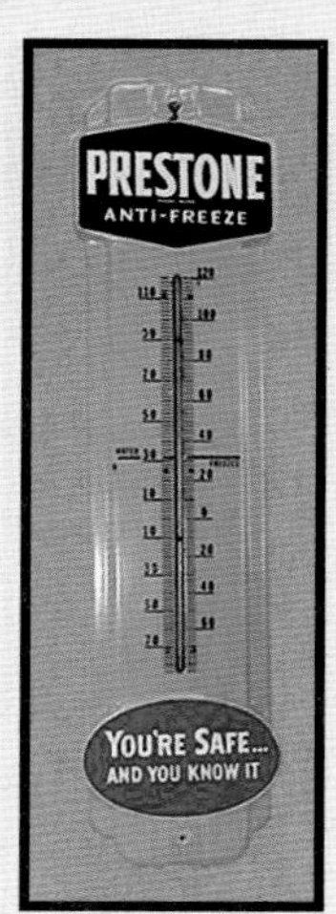

Prestone, 1940s, porcelain, $200.00.

Sun Crest, 1950s, round, $250.00.

Yellowstone Bourbon Whiskey, 1960s, box, $100.00.

Sauer's Extracts, 1920s, $500.00.

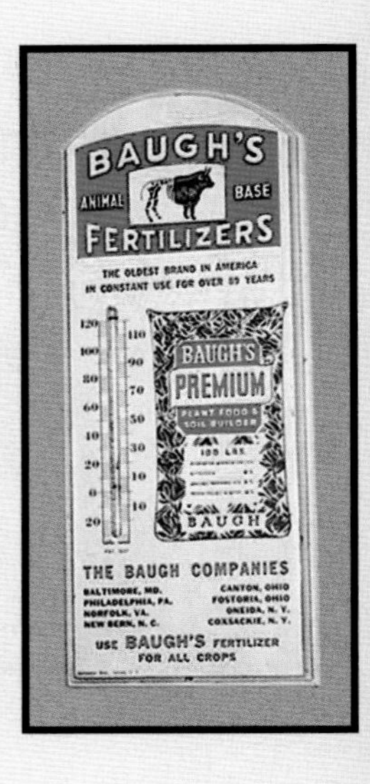

Baugh's Fertilizers, 1950s, wooden, $100.00.

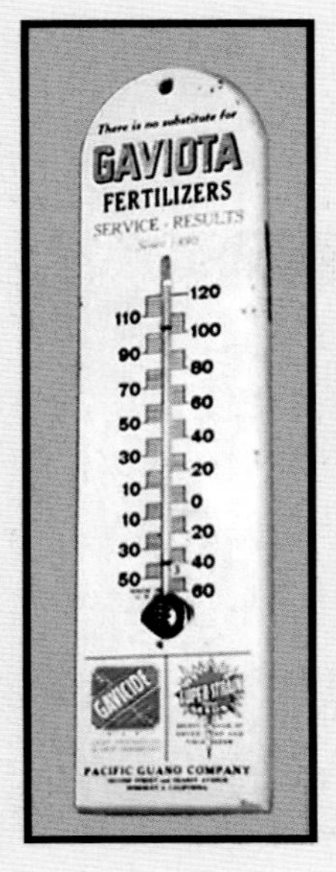

Gaviota Fertilizers, 1950s, wooden, $100.00.

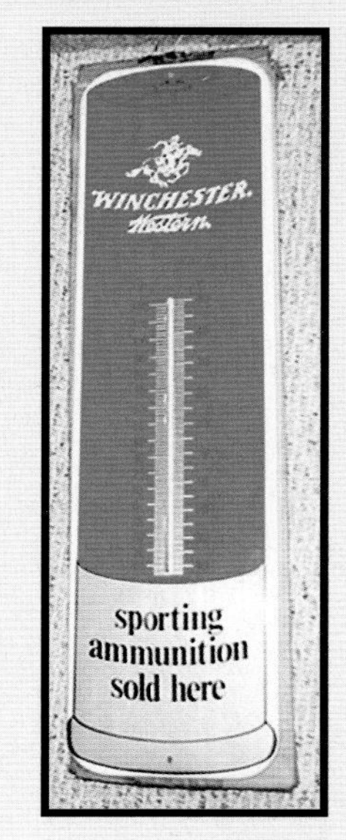

Winchester Sporting Ammunition, 1970s, orange, $125.00.

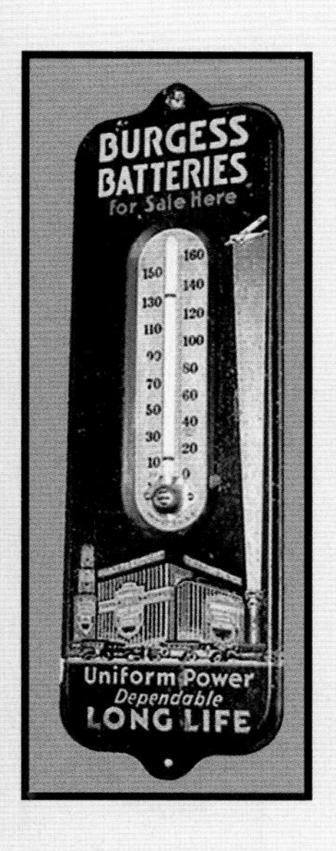

Burgess Batteries, 1940s, $300.00.

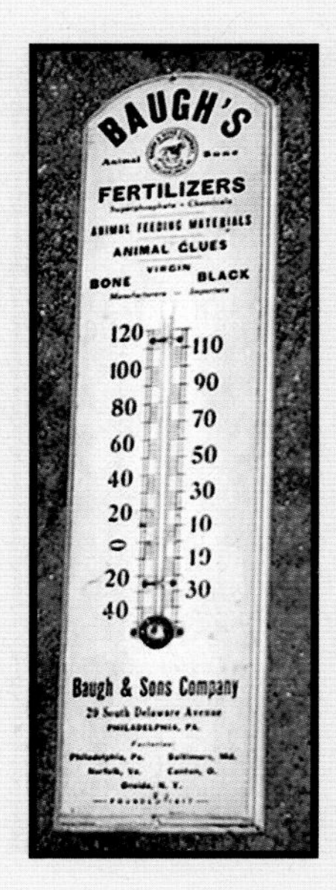

Baugh's Fertilizers, 1940s, wooden, $200.00.

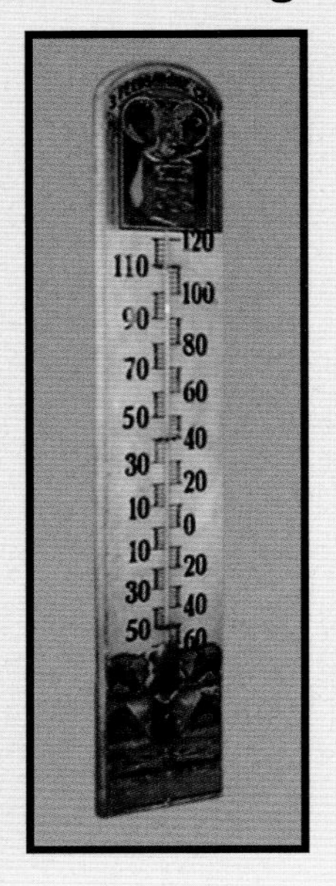

International Livestock, early 1920s, $1,000.00.

Universal Batteries, 1930s, porcelain, $300.00.

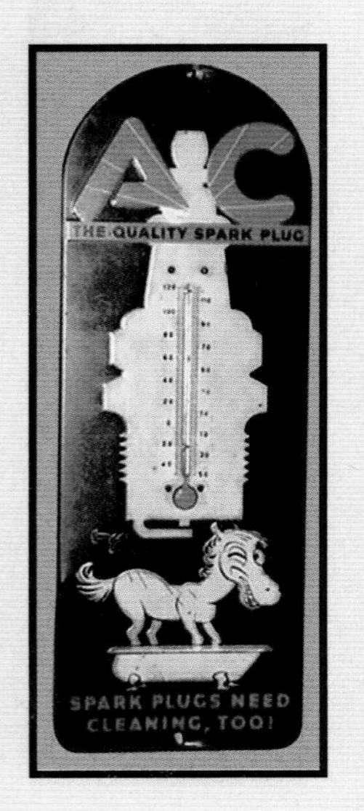

A C Delco, 1950s, $500.00.

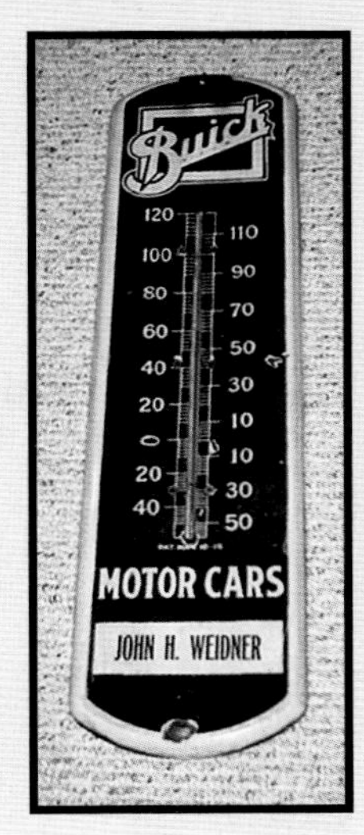

Buick Motor Cars, 1915 – 1920, porcelain, $300.00.

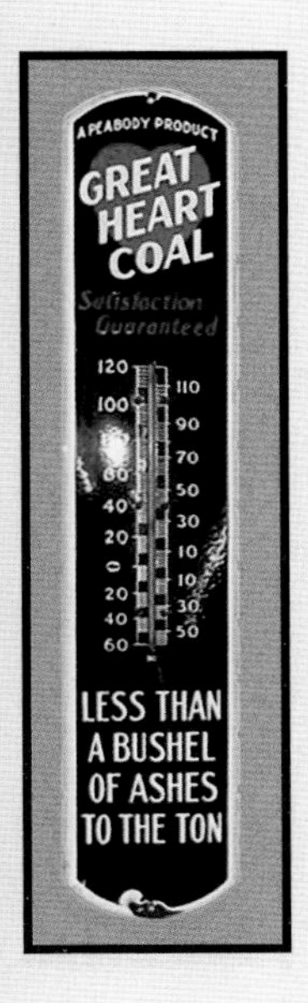

Great Heart Coal, c. 1916, porcelain, $350.00.

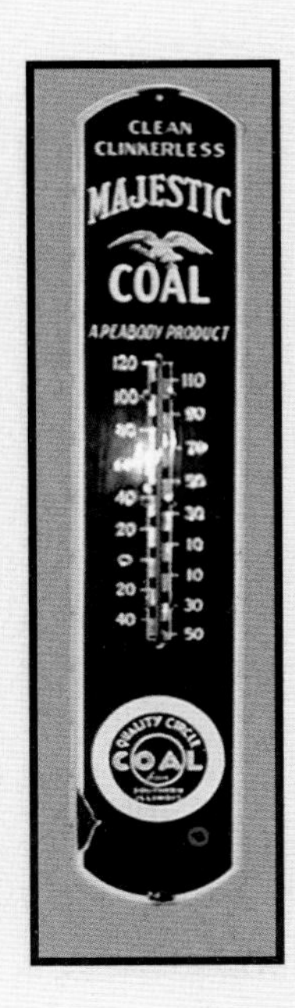

Majestic Coal, c. 1915, $300.00.

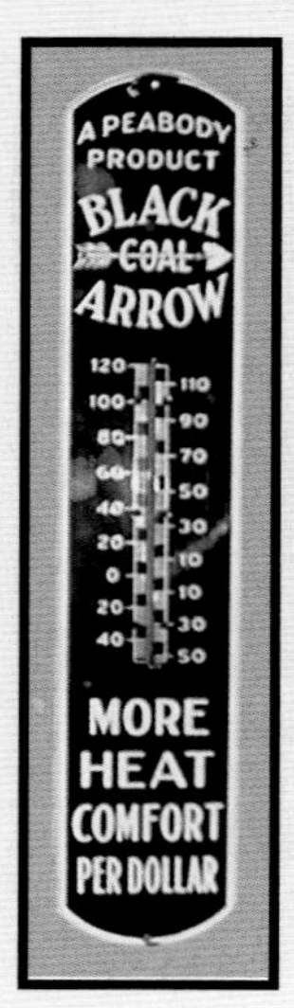

Black Arrow Coal, c. 1915, $300.00.

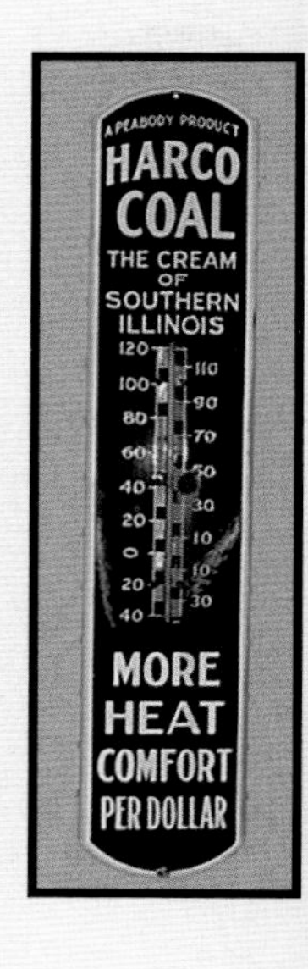

Harco Coal, c. 1915, $300.00.

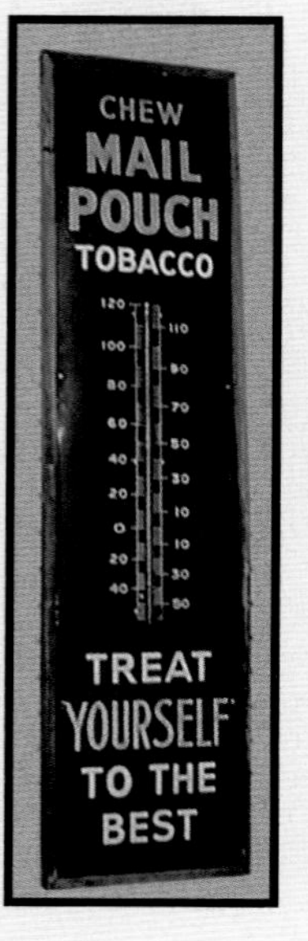

Mail Pouch, c. 1920, porcelain, six feet in length, $800.00.

U.S.S. American Fence, c. 1915, porcelain, $150.00.

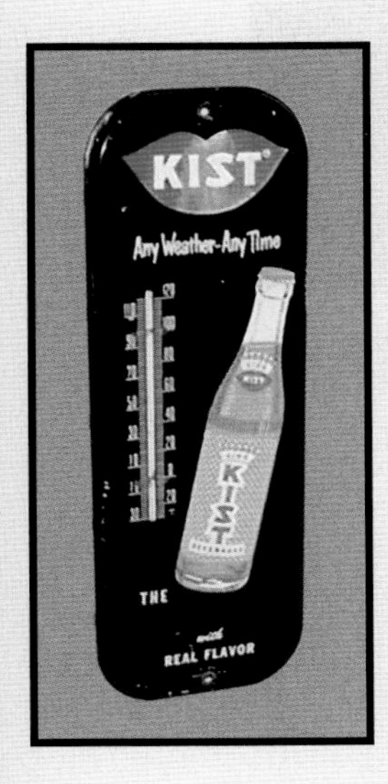

Kist Soda, 1960s, lips and bottle, $150.00.

Bubble Up, 1960s, double caps, $150.00.

Boy Scouts Collectibles

A photograph of a group of Eagle Scouts and their leader (c. 1920s).

Philip Edwards has been a serious collector of Boy Scouts related memorabilia for more than 20 years. He initially became involved in Boy Scouts as a participant in 1939.

Mr. Edwards has graciously provided this section and allowed us to photograph a portion of his extensive collection. We are in his debt.

Mr. Edwards can be reached by e-mail at pedwar@verizon.net.

I have been in scouting since 1939 when I joined the Cub Scouts. As a Cub Scout, the family is a major participant. Activities (day camp, trips to local attractions, and ball games) were also important. Den and Pack meetings prepared the Cub for the next level. My experiences as a Cub were positive and in 1942, when I was 12 years old, I joined the Boy Scouts.

The scout years were filled with extended camping trips, merit badge work, and advancement in rank. Most memorable were the three years when I spent four weeks each summer at Boxwell Boy Scout Camp located on the Harpeth River in Tennessee. There, and at school and home, I earned the merit badges I needed to obtain the Eagle rank in 1946. The most notable achievements during those years were the Eagle rank, senior patrol leader, my selection by my camping peers as dining room director, and also being "tapped" into the Order of the Arrow.

After college, Air Force duty, graduate school, work, and family, I returned to scouting in 1983 as Scoutmaster and Round Table Commissioner. I attended the World Jamboree in Canada that same year and in 1985 earned the beads for Wood Badge. In 1988 I took my troop to Philmont Scout Ranch in New Mexico where we spent 12 days hiking in the desert and the mountains.

It was at the World Jamboree that I was introduced to collecting Boy Scouts memorabilia. There was much swapping and trading. Presently I attend seven to eight swapping sessions each year to extend my collection. These sessions (Trade-o-Res) are held in various towns in the Midwest. I also make use of eBay to obtain memorabilia in addition to selling my duplicates.

The Scout movement was started in 1908 in Great Britain by Sir Robert Baden-Powell. Scouting was brought to the United States by W.D. Boyce of Ottawa, Illinois, and Chicago in 1910. The popularity of scouting, which matched its activities with the interests of youth, was immediate. The program was granted a federal charter in 1916. Over the years 110 million boys have belonged to the Boy Scouts. More than one million have earned the Eagle rank.

Countless political leaders, sports figures, CEOs, astronauts, and a former President of the United States (Gerald Ford) have earned the Eagle rank.

The appeal of collecting scout memorabilia is the realization that much of the early badges, pins, and uniforms were worn by boys and men living in the 1910s and 1920s and by the early leaders — Baden-Powell, James West, and W.D. Boyce. As the movement advanced into the 1930s, other leaders and boys earned and wore what is called memorabilia today. One is merely documenting the history of the Scout movement through memorabilia. Today's boys are collecting and preserving post-WWII scout activities, primarily patches. As they grow older, earlier material will exert a powerful attraction.

Some hints for the collector of BSA merchandise:

1. There are various methods that can assist in dating an item:
   a. Note the address of the BSA headquarters as this has changed over the years.
   b. Know the dates when a certain manufacturer was used by BSA.
   c. Use manufacturer markings (these are rare) on metal items (please note that "Pat 1911" on the back of a metal has no bearing as to date of issue or use).
   d. Use literature such as *A Guide to Dating and Identifying BSA Badges, Uniforms, and Insignia.*
2. The edge of a patch can be either cut edge or rolled edge. The cut edge patch is earlier, existing up to the mid-1950s.
3. Many patches have been reproduced with only a smattering of documentation so it pays to know and trust your dealer.
4. Many early toys were not authorized by BSA. They are still very collectible.
5. Over the years, there have been many books written about many aspects of scouting memorabilia. Building an extensive library is very useful.
6. There are several outstanding collector-oriented organizations that one can join to increase knowledge about BSA memorabilia.
7. Visit the excellent "brick and mortar" scouting museums around the USA as well as Boy Scout museum sites on the Internet.
8. Contact your local scout office to find the location and dates for Trad-O-Res in your area.
9. Enjoy your collecting.

YIS (Yours in Scouting)
Philip Edwards

Mr. Edwards's uniform.

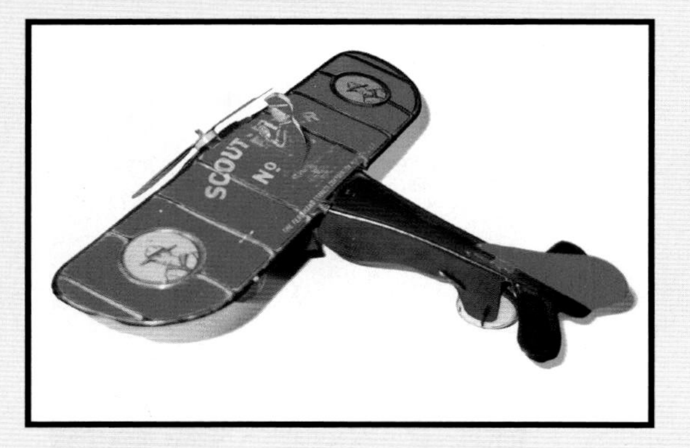

Scout Flyer No. 48, Strauss Corp., c. 1915, $600.00.

Peanut butter tin, Bayle Food Products Co., 1915 – 1920, $400.00.

Official Boy Scout shoes, Brown Shoe Co., 1930s, $75.00.

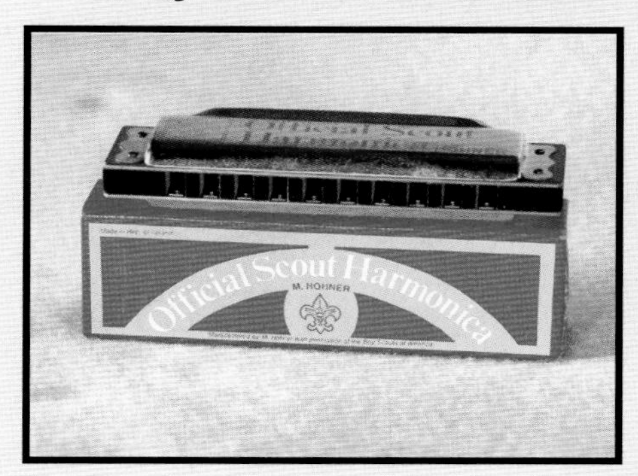

Boy Scout harmonica with box, 1960s, $25.00.

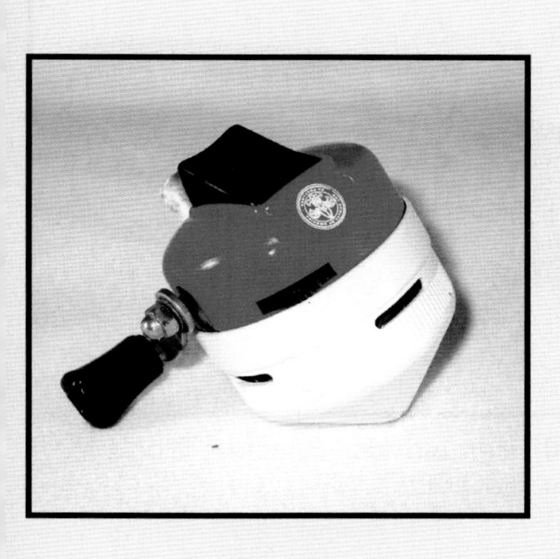

Fishing reel, 1967 – 1970s, $50.00.

Official Boy Scout whistle, 1950s – 1960s, plastic, $25.00.

Batteries for signal sets, 1950s – 1960s, almost never with set, $40.00.

Official first aid kit, Bauer & Block, c. 1920s, $60.00.

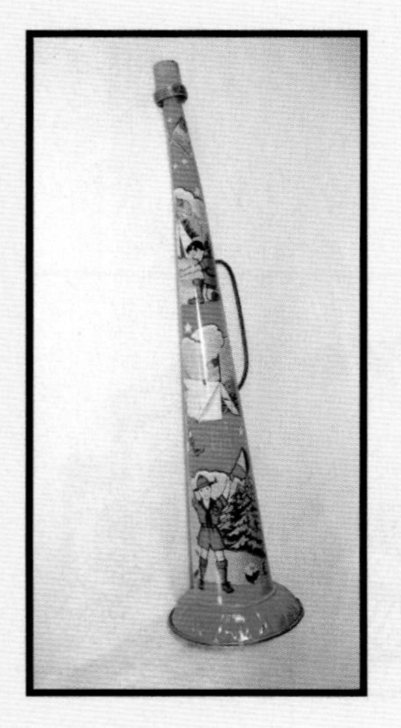

Boy Scout horn, 1930s, unofficial, $95.00.

Boy Scout drums unofficial, approximately 6" to 11" diameters, 1908 – 1920, from top to bottom: $150.00, $150.00, $150.00, $200.00, $300.00.

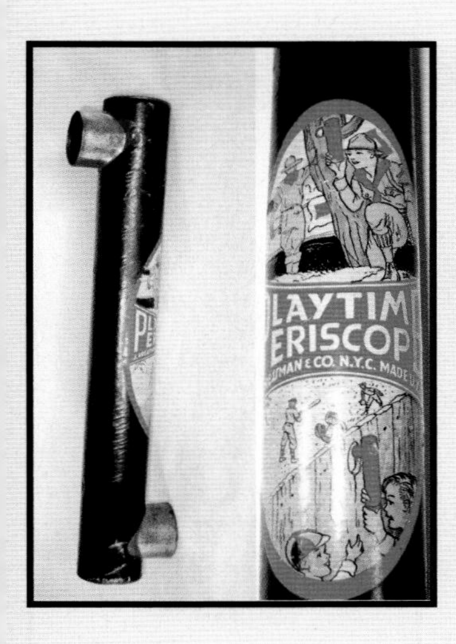

Boy Scout periscope, 1920s, unofficial, $110.00.

Saluting Scout calendar, 1927, $40.00.

Official paperweight from the National Jamboree, 1937, $55.00.

Boy Scout blocks, 1940s, $60.00.

Register and Vote poster, 1952, $35.00.

Block set, German, 1915 – 1925, $400.00.

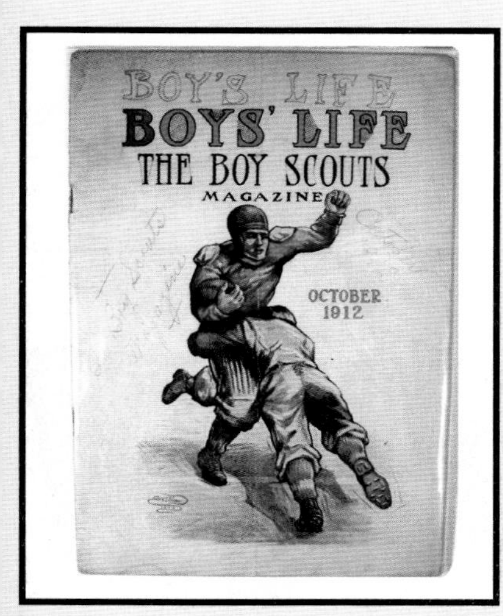

Boys' Life, October 1912, $150.00.

The Cat Scouts, Wain and Pope, 1927, $400.00.

Official Cook Kit #1200, 1930s – 1950, $25.00.

Indian Handicraft Set, 1940 – 1950s, $30.00.

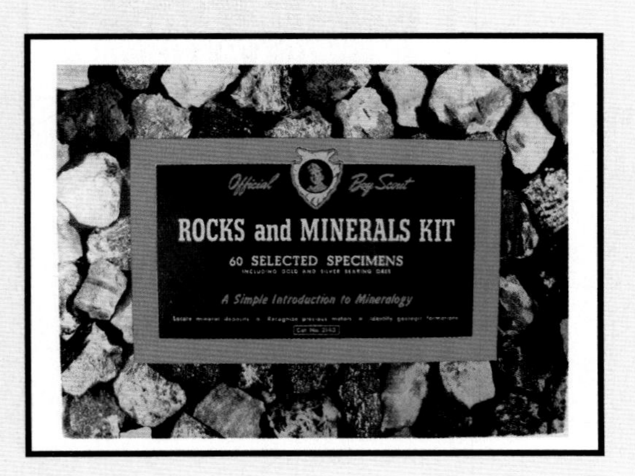

Rock & Minerals Kit, #2143, c. 1940s, $30.00.

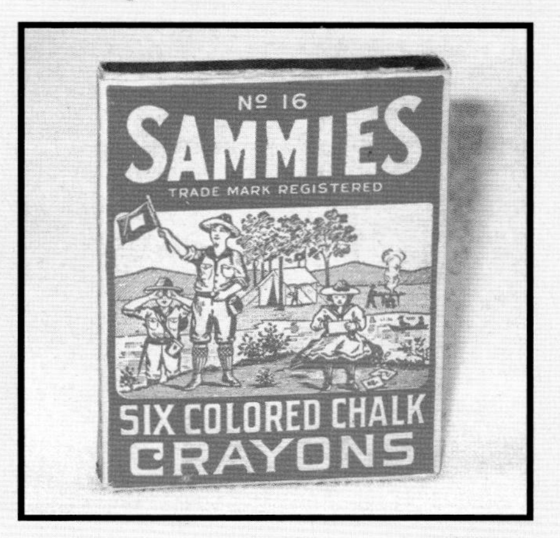

Boy Scout chalk crayons, 1920s, #16, $40.00.

Official binoculars, c. 1960s, $25.00.

Baden-Powell pitcher, c. 1908, $300.00.

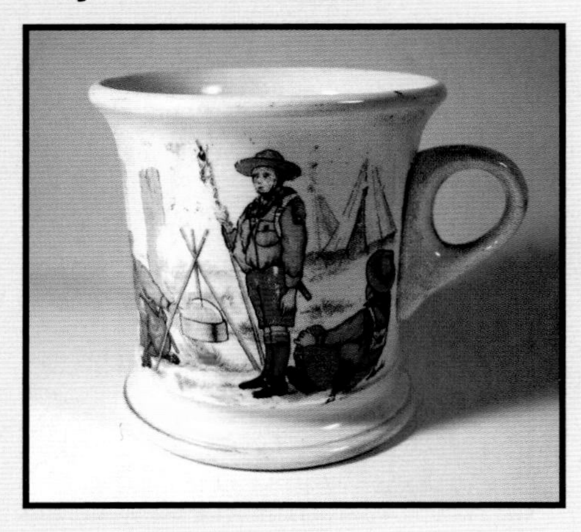

Mug, T.P.C. & Co., German, 1912 – 1915, $200.00.

Scout bookends, c. 1930s, $75.00 (pair).

Seneca Scout camera, 1915, unofficial, #2, $100.00.
#3 Seneca Scout camera, 1915, unofficial, $100.00.

Drinking cup, c. 1915, $50.00.

Bicycle bell, c. 1910 – 1919, $75.00.

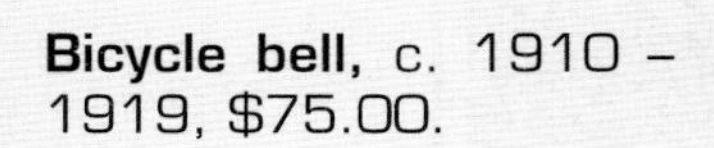

Bicycle bell, c. 1910 – 1919, $75.00.

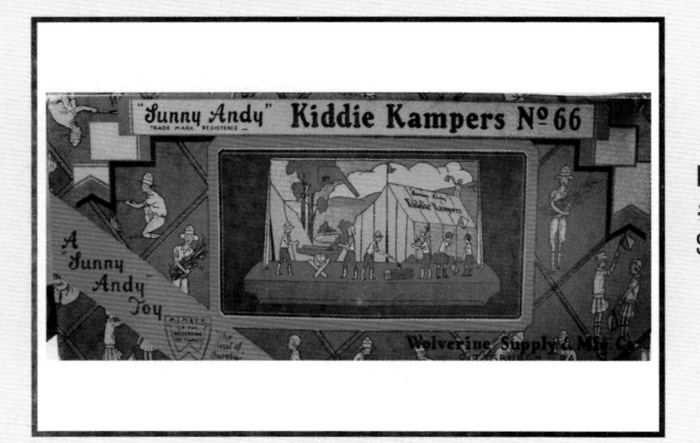

Kiddie Kampers #66 box, c. 1930s, $200.00.

Kiddie Kampers wind-up set, Wolverine Supply, $600.00 (box & wind-up set).

Marx Boy Scout camp playset, c. 1950s, $600.00.

Tin toy "Kiddie Kamp," gravity operation, Wolverine Supply, c. 1930s, $400.00.

Boy Scouts in Camp #5850, McLaughlin Bros., c. 1912 – 1915, $300.00.

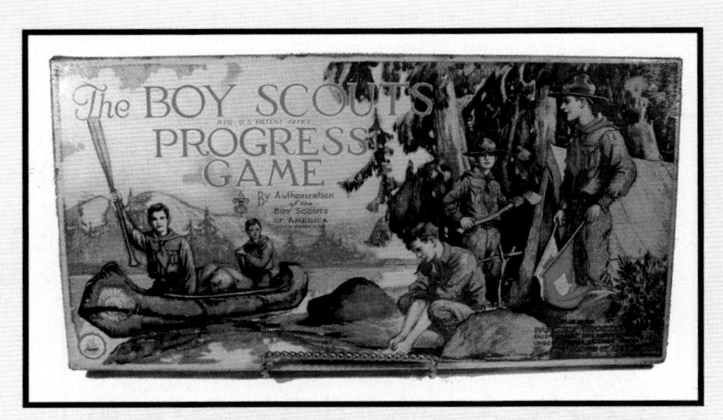

The Boy Scouts' Progress Game, Parker Brothers, 1924, $200.00.

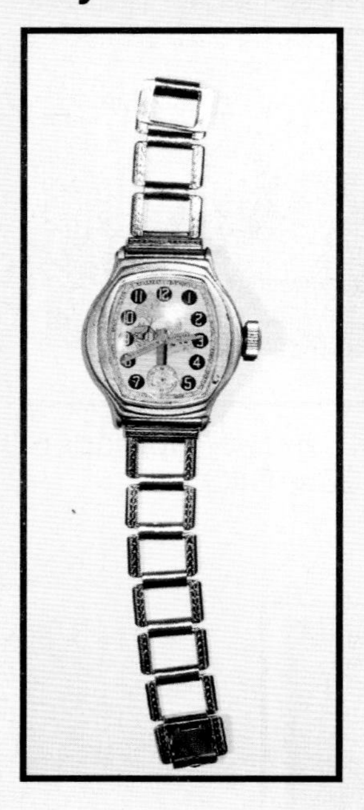

Ingersoll wrist watch, 1930s, $200.00.

Ingersoll pocket watch, c. 1930s, $300.00.

Lotto game, Bo Scout Edition, c 1920s, $75.00.

A Scout Is Courteous box with handkerchief, c. 1915, $110.00.

A Scout Is Friendly box with handkerchief, c. 1915, $110.00.

"Boy Scout" cap gun, c. 1930s, $200.00.

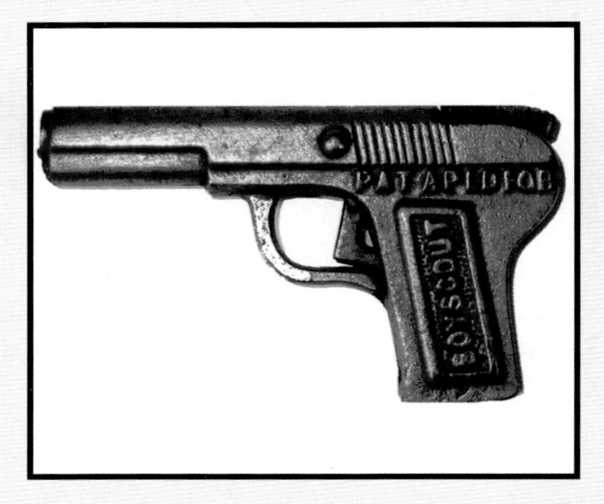

Boy Scout machine gun, Kilgore Mgt. Co., Homestead, PA, 1913, $600.00.

1933 World Jamboree knife, Scout shop souvenir, brass, $400.00.

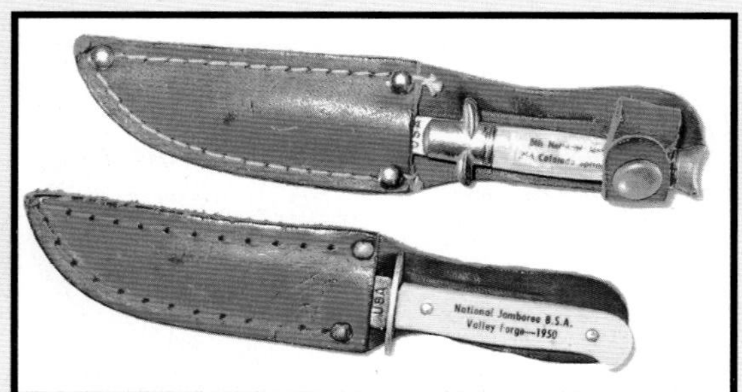

1960 National Jamboree souvenir knife, $35.00.
1950 National Jamboree souvenir knife, $50.00.

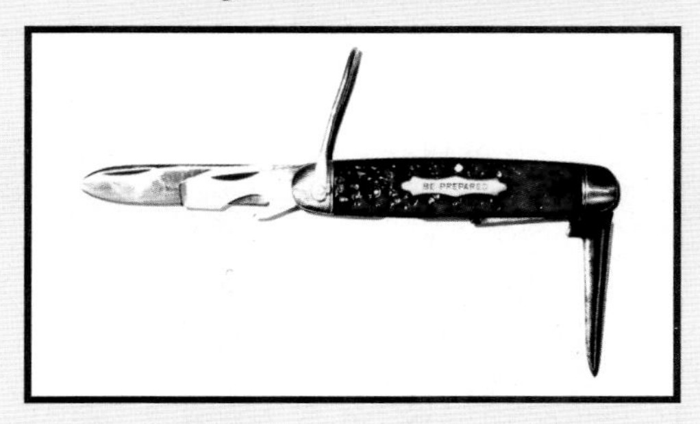

New York Knife Co. first official Boy Scouts of America knife, 1911 – 1916, $400.00.

First class patrol leader patch, c. 1915 – 1925, $200.00.
First class scribe patch, c. 1916 – 1925, $400.00.

Assistant Scoutmaster patch, 1920 – 1937, $150.00.
Assistant Scoutmaster patch, 1911 – 1920, $300.00.

Subcamp VII 1937 World Jamboree patch, U.S. contingent camp, $900.00.

Subcamp Bourgoone 1947 World Jamboree patch, U.S. contingent, camp, $900.00.

Philturn patch, Rocky Mountain Scout Camp, 1940s (reproductions of this patch are known), $600.00.

Left: Region 7 patch, 1940 – 1941, $600.00.

Right: Region 7 patch, mid- to late-1940s, $200.00.

Enterprise No. 12, 32" high, 25" wheels, original American eagle decals (transfers), $1,700.00 – 1,900.00.

Coffee Mills

Coffee mills were designed for use on the wall, in the lap, on the counter, or on the floor. If a mill is to retain significant value it *must* maintain its original surface, labels or decals, all parts in working order, base, and drawer. If it has been repainted, relabeled or re-decaled, and had new parts made for it, somewhere there has to be a better example for your collection.

Keep in mind that coffee mills were certainly decorative but their primary function was utilitarian. Most were in daily use and suffered from the experience. Few survived without varying blemishes and bruises. The owner's primary concern was the mill's ability and willingness to grind the coffee.

The mills illustrated and priced here are assumed to be in original condition. The values reflect their rarity.

Enterprise cast-iron wall mill, c. 1890, $700.00 – 850.00

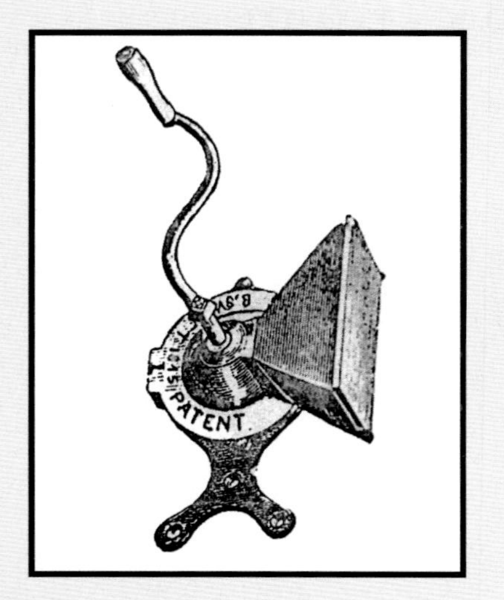

Lane Brothers side mill, made by Swift, 1845 – 1922, $400.00 – 700.00.

Logan and Strowbridg, 1876 – 1904, $375.00 – 500.00.

LaLance and Gosjean mill no. 65, c. 1890, $400.00 – 600.00.

Waddell lap mill, 1889 – 1892, $400.00 – 600.00.

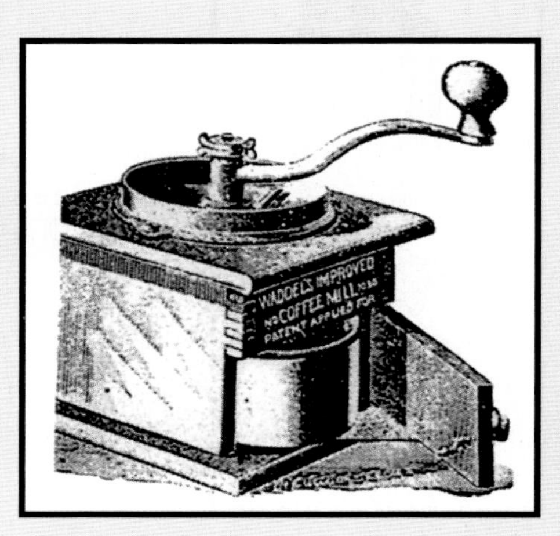

Toy coffee mills, late 1880s – 1930s, $300.00 – 450.00 (each).

Arcade mill No. 257, c. 1900, $300.00 – 500.00.

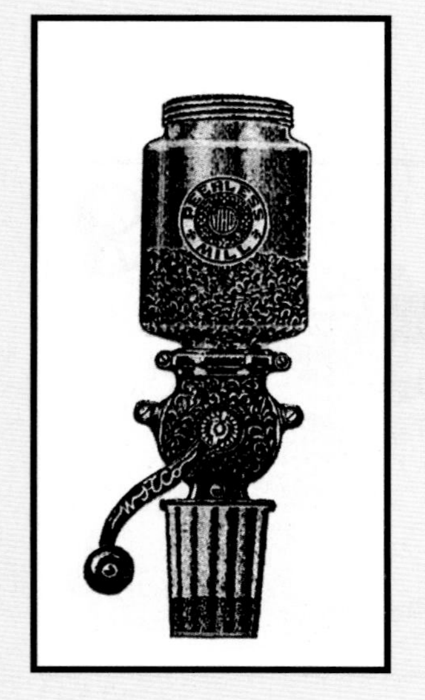

Wrightsville Hardware Co. Peerless Mill, c. 1915, $550.00 – 675.00.

Norton Bros. canister mill, c. 1887, $750.00 – 950.00.

Arcade "Telephone Mill" No. 1, early 1900s, $1,500.00 – 2,500.00.

Bronson and Walton mill, Silver Lake, 1905 – 1915, $500.00 – 600.00.

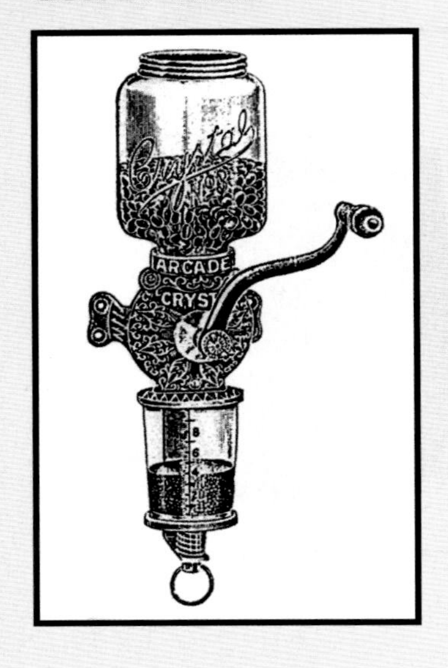

Arcade art deco mill, No. 9010, 1920s, $700.00 – 950.00.

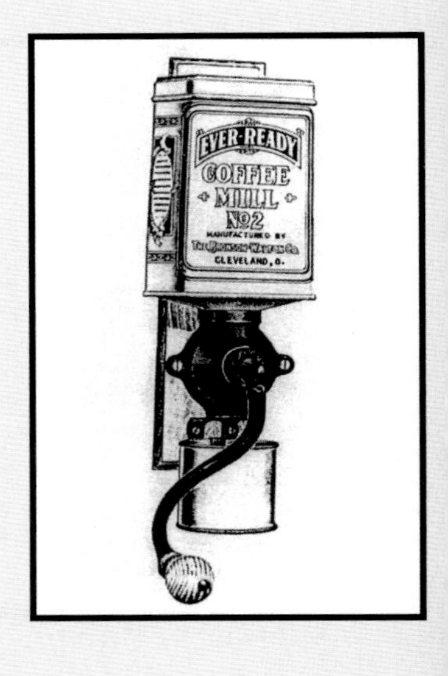

Bronson and Walton mill, No. 2, Ever-Ready, c. 1910, $600.00 – 700.00.

Coles counter mill, 1891 – 1910, $1,500.00 – 2,500.00.

Enterprise mill #2, 1873 – 1920, $1,500.00 – 2,500.00.

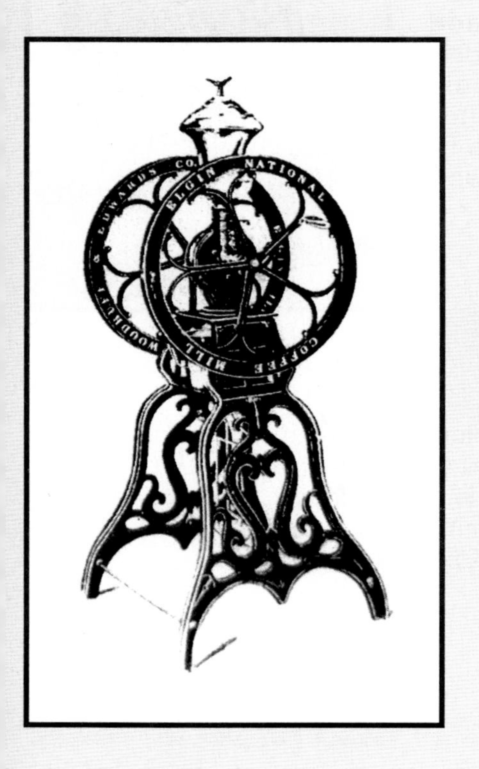

Woodruff and Edwards floor mill, 1890 – 1910, $3,000.00 – 4,500.00.

Coffee Mills

The Grand Union Tea Company was created in 1877. Eventually the company had its own grocery stores and several thousand salesmen selling their products from horsedrawn wagons door to door across America. They gave away or offered as premiums two wall coffee mills and sold this example. Adding to its value is that it was made for Grand Union by the Griswold Manufacturing Company. $500.00 – 750.00.

John Hoffman "Old Time" blended roasted coffee from Milwaukee, Wisconsin. The mill was made by Arcade Manufacturing of Freeport, Illinois. The Hoffman mill dates from c. 1915. They were offered as premiums by the John Hoffman Company. $375.00 – 450.00.

National coffee mill, original paint and eagle finial, c. 1910, made by C. Parker Company of Meriden, Connecticut, $1,200.00 – 1,600.00.

L F & C, New Britain, Conn., iron hopper, original paint. Landers, Frary, and Clark made mills comparable to the Enterprise Company of Philadelphia. This #11 mill had a hopper capacity of four ounces and is 12½" tall. It was made after 1890 when the Enterprise patents ran out. It dates from about 1900 and was a table model for use at home. $375.00 – 500.00.

Landers, Frary, and Clark wheeled mill, iron hopper, wooden drawer, 10¾" wheels, original paint and decals (transfers), c. 1905. $1,500.00 – 1,800.00.

Enterprise #2, Philadelphia, Pa., made between 1871 and 1873, 9" wheel diameter, rare form, maple handle grip, $2,000.00 – 2,500.00.

Enterprise No. 12, 32" high, 25" wheels, original American eagle decals (transfers), weighs 120 pounds, $1,700.00 – 1,900.00.

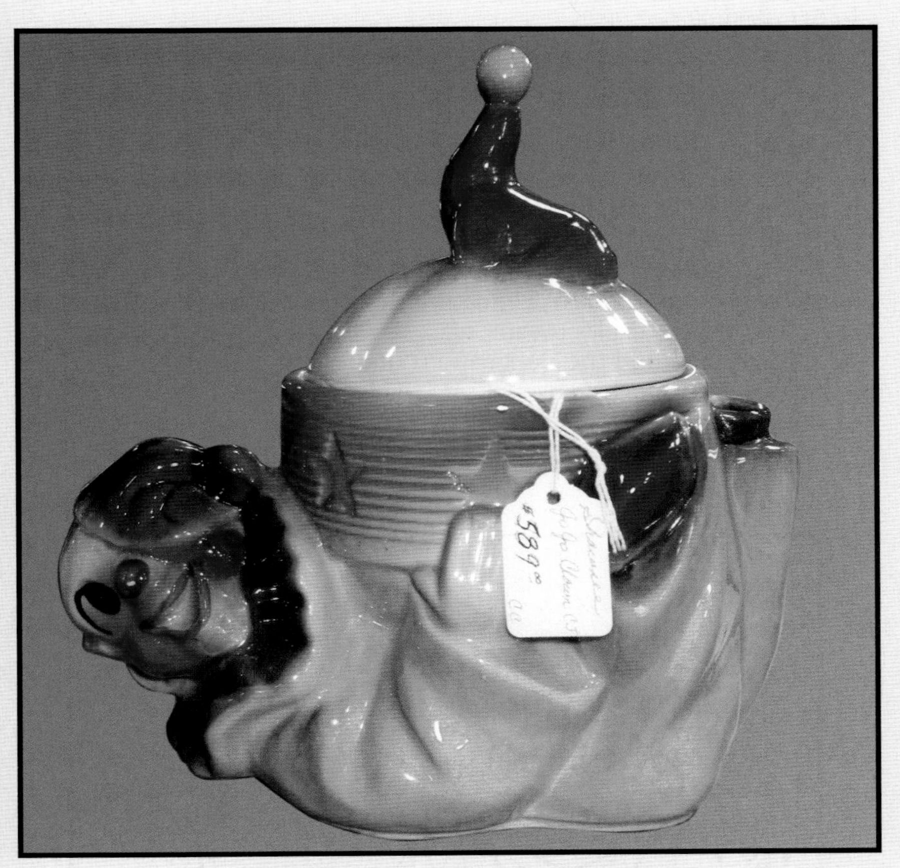

JoJo the Clown, Shawnee, $589.00.

Cookie Jars

Cookie Jars date back to the early 1930s and were mostly imported from Japan. During WW II "Buy American" campaigns were conducted, German and Japanese items such as post cards and cookie jars were taken off the shelves. Shawnee pottery among others took over the growing market. Corner dime stores, Woolworth's, and Sears Roebuck all carried the popular American made cookie jars.

The first cookie jar Shawnee released was the "Smiley the Pig." They came with either a blue or red scarf and were offered at the wholesale price of $1.00 each (by the dozen). Smiley Pig, Winnie Pig, Muggsy the Dog, Puss n' Boots, and Dutch Jack and Jill were the most popular jars produced by the Shawnee Pottery. Smiley, in his many variations, is one of the most "desired" jars of all for cookie jar collectors.

Early jars were cold painted meaning they were painted after they had gone through the kiln. Unfortunatly, after multiple washings, the cold paint was literally swept off the jar along with much of the value. Later jars had the decoration "under" the glaze and the painted surface was preserved.

Smiley patent drawing.

What To Look For

Cookie jars with gold trim are always at a premium. Most gold-trimmed jars were originally seconds or had blemishes; gold and decals were applied to the jars to hide the blemish. These jars were later sold in specialty shops at a higher price than the dime-store models. Another rarity among Shawnee Pig cookie jars features strawberry decals — the flowered cookie jars are much more common. When examining cookie jars look for hairline cracks in the jars and always check the lid for cracks and chips which also diminish value. Understand the difference between a "craze" and a crack. A "craze" typically is a break in the glaze and is a long way from being a crack.

Marks

There are several different marks used on Shawnee cookie jars, including "U.S.A." by itself; "Patented/Smiley Co./Shawnee/U.S.A."; "Patented Winnie/Shawnee/USA/61"; "Patented/Mugsey/USA"; "Patented/Winnie/USA"; "USA/6; and Patented/Puss N Boots/USA." Shawnee's most popular line of decorative art pottery was the Corn King series.

The golden age of selling cookie jars took place at the Andy Warhol auction at Sotheby's, April 23 – May 3, 1988, in New York City. There were 155 cookie jars in 38 lots that sold for a total of $247,830 (in 1988 dollars). The jars were estimated realistically at $25.00 – 50.00 each. Several members of the audience estimated that a duplicate collection could be put together for less than $5,000.00. The only difference in the $5,000.00 jars was that Warhol had not owned them and Sotheby's had not attached a Warhol sticker to each one that was offered at auction.

Warhol's 74 pieces of Fiesta dinnerware sold for $5,500.00. The pre-auction estimate was about $20.00 per piece. There was a 10% buyer's premium.

The cookie jars pictured are a variety of early cookie jars recently sold at the 3rd Sunday Market from a collection owned by Sue Herron and her sister-in-law Sue Cox in Bloomington, Illinois.

Smiley the Pig with yellow scarf, Shawnee, $425.00.

Smiley the Pig with red scarf and tulips, Shawnee, $315.00.

Smiley the Pig, Shawnee, cold painted, $75.00.

Polka-Dot Pig, Shawnee, $75.00.

Mr. Pig, Shawnee, cold painted, $55.00.

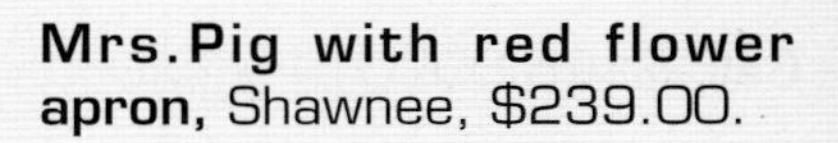

Mrs.Pig with red flower apron, Shawnee, $239.00.

Girl Pig with pink apron, American Bisque, $200.00.

Girl Pig, Shawnee, cold painted with red flower, $195.00.

Cat, $125.00.

Bear, polka-dot, $100.00.

Bear, polka-dot, $100.00.

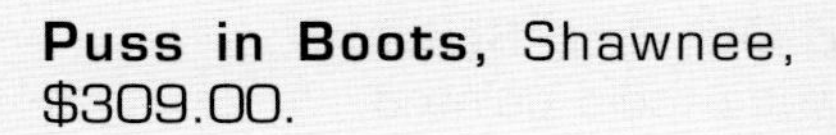

Puss in Boots, Shawnee, $309.00.

Puss in Boots, Shawnee, lid chipped, $200.00.

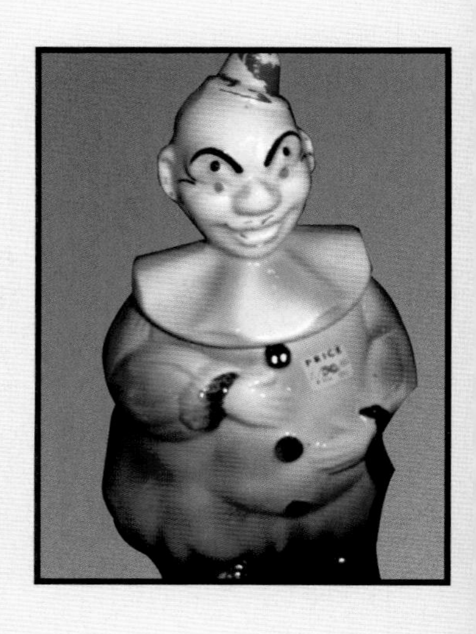

Clown, $400.00.

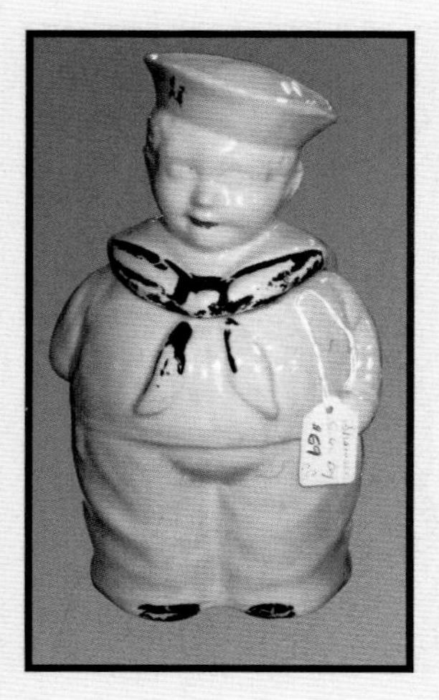

Good Old Boy, Sailor, Shawnee, cold painted, $69.00.

Mugsy the Dog, Shawnee, $480.00.

Old Lady, American Bisque, $200.00.

Baby Chick with hat, American Bisque, $80.00.

Fishing Lures

Jitterbug, Fred Arbogast Co., Akron, OH; plastic-lipped, WW II era, perch, excellent plus condition, $40.00 – 50.00.

This section was contributed by Bobby Farling, a renowned Northwoods guide, campfire chef, and horsemen. Mr. Farling also has an extensive collection of fishing lures.

The hobby of collecting fishing tackle has been growing steadily for many years. Fishing is certainly among the most popular outdoor activities in America. It seems only natural that people who enjoy fishing would have an interest in learning about and collecting antique fishing tackle. This might include lures, flies, rods, reels, and numerous fishing-related items.

There are scores of reference books currently available to collectors which cover various aspects of the hobby. There are also organized clubs which promote the hobby, sponsor shows in various regions of the country, and provide valuable information to their members. The shows also enable collectors to meet other people with similar collecting interests. Some of the major clubs include:

1. NFLCC — National Fishing Lure Collectors Club (www.nflcc.net)
2. ORCA — Old Reel Collectors Assn. (www.orcaonline.org)
3. FATC — Florida Antique Tackle Collectors (www.fatc.net)

Many factors influence the value of a lure: true scarcity of a particular lure, in terms of how many were made; the color, of which many manufacturers offered a variety to choose from; and very importantly, condition. The closer to mint condition, the more the value will be enhanced. Every paint chip, hook drag, worm burn, cracked eye, and other imperfection can greatly affect the value of the lure.

My personal interests are Florida baits by any number of makers, Paw Paw lures, Jamison Wig-L-Twins, and Clark Water Scouts. I am always interested in adding lures in excellent condition to my collection. I can be reached via e-mail at: bonefish8@centurytel.net.

Arnold Tackle Corp., Paw Paw, Michigan

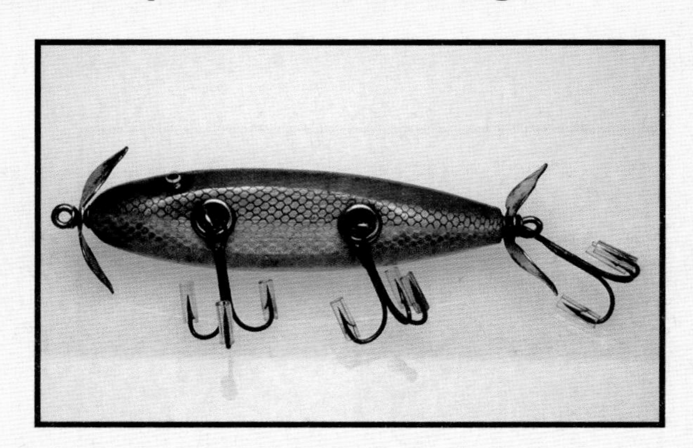

Injured Minnow, excellent plus condition, $35.00 – 45.00.

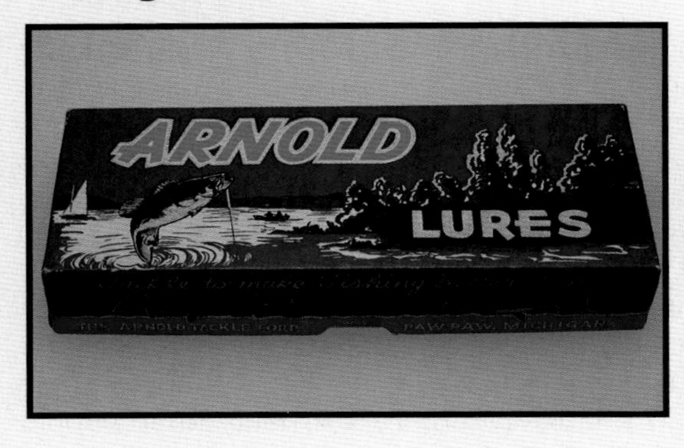

Two-piece cardboard box, excellent plus condition, $25.00 – 30.00.

Florida Fishing Tackle Mfg. Co., St. Petersburg, Florida

Florida Shad, cup-rigged (early), excellent condition, $25.00 – 35.00.

Pop-Eyed Frog, excellent plus condition, $75.00 – 100.00.

Tipsy Cuda, Frog Scale, excellent plus condition, $65.00 – 85.00.

Twitchin' Cuda, blue-green, excellent plus condition, rare color, $100.00 – 150.00.

Two-piece cardboard box, excellent plus condition, circa 1934, $50.00 – 80.00.

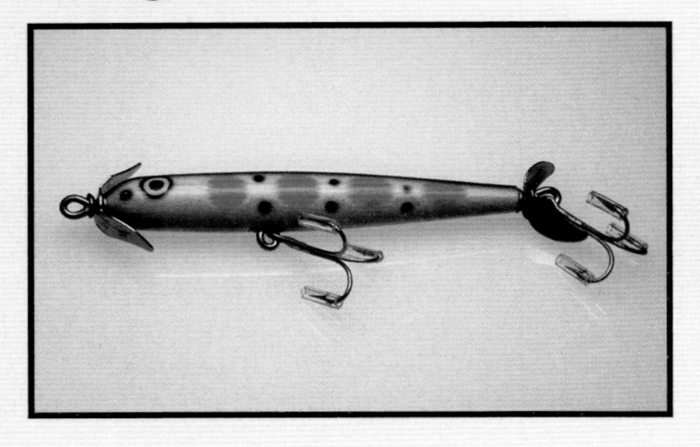

Slim Twin Cuda, Christmas Tree, cup-rigged (early), excellent plus condition, $50.00 – 75.00.

Baby Florida Shiner, cup-rigged (early), ceramic eyes, excellent plus condition, $25.00 – 35.00.

Florida Shiner, cup-rigged (early), in two-piece plastic box with insert, painted eyes, excellent condition, $35.00 – 45.00.

Dalton Special #547 Shad, excellent plus condition, $20.00 – 25.00.

Marine Metal Products Co., Clearwater, Florida

Medium Dalton Special, #546 NP, natural perch, new in cardboard box with plastic window, $15.00 – 20.00.

Biff Bait Co., Milwaukee, Wisconsin

Master Biff, yellow with black spots, excellent condition, $60.00 – 80.00.

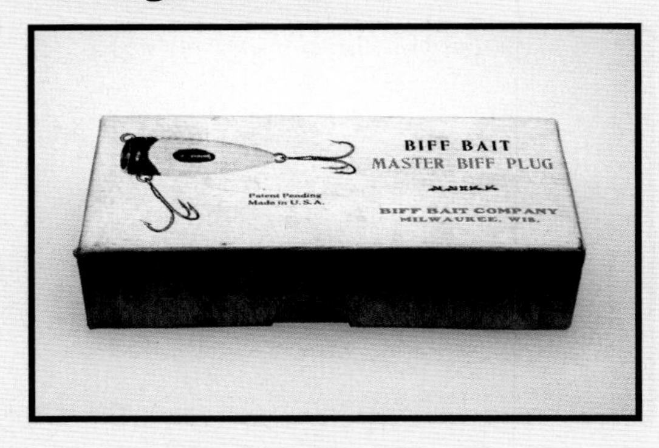

Two-piece cardboard box, excellent plus condition, $90.00 – 110.00.

Bingo Bait Co., Corpus Christi, Texas

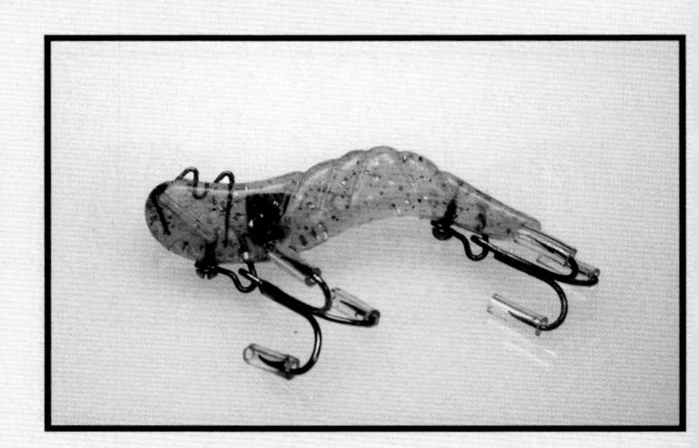

Plugging Shorty Shrimp, yellow with glitter, excellent plus condition, $10.00 – 15.00.

Bite-Em Bate Co., Ft. Wayne, Indiana

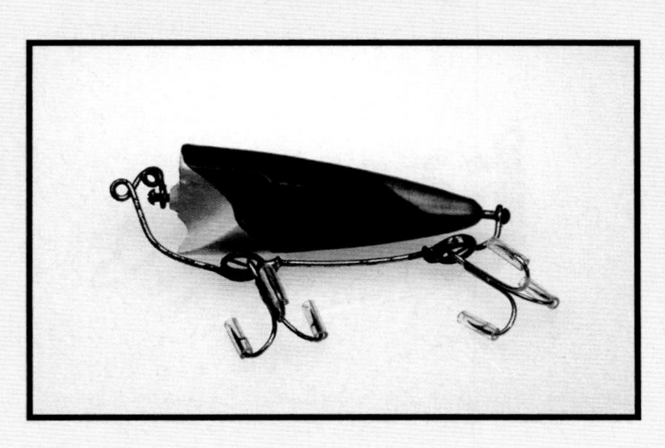

Bite-Em Bate, white/black/gold, excellent plus condition, $100.00 – 125.00.

Boone Bait Co., Winter Park, Florida

Spinana, blue mullet, excellent plus condition, $15.00 – 20.00.

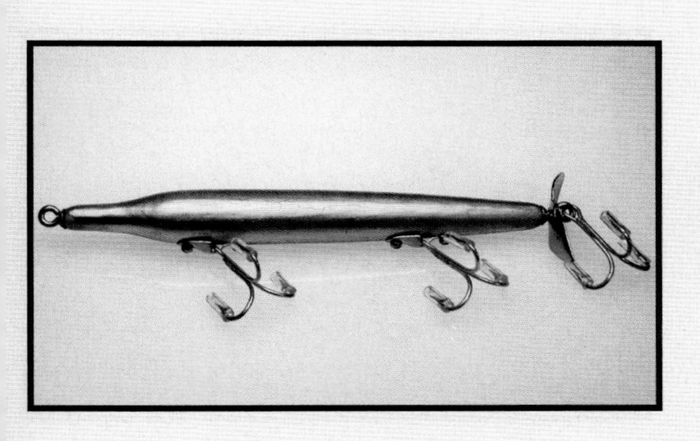

Needlefish, gold, excellent condition, $15.00 – 25.00.

Buckeye Bait Corp., Council Grove, Kansas

Bug-N-Bait, rainbow trout, excellent plus condition, $75.00 – 125.00 (rare color).

C.A. Clark Co., Springfield, Missouri

Water Scout, dent eye (early), yellow perch, excellent plus condition, $100.00 – 125.00.

Water Scout #327, white/silver ribs/red scale, excellent plus condition, rare color, $40.00 – 60.00.

Two-piece cardboard box, excellent plus condition, $15.00 – 25.00.

Creek Chub Bait Co., Garrett, Indiana

Plunker #3225, white scale, excellent plus condition, rare color, $350.00 – 450.00.

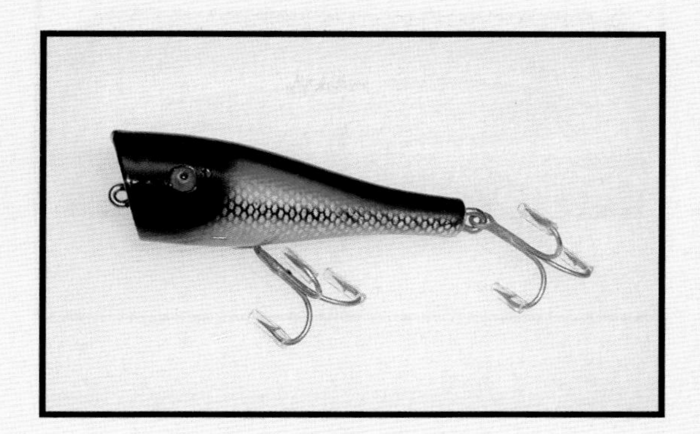

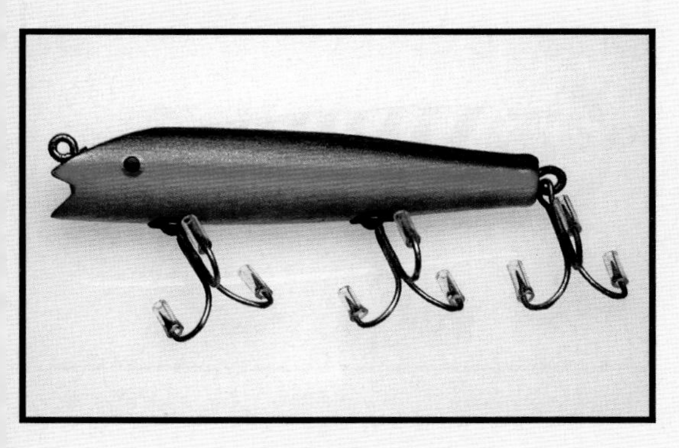

Darter #2008, rainbow, excellent plus condition, $50.00 – 75.00.

Eger Bait Manufacturing Co., Bartow, Florida

#113 Weedless Dillinger, excellent condition, $25.00 – 30.00.

#207 Junior Dillinger, plastic top cardboard box, excellent plus condition, $30.00 – 40.00.

#301 Master Dillinger, painted eyes, excellent plus condition, $20.00 – 30.00.

#301 Master Dillinger, painted tack eyes, excellent plus condition, $40.00 – 60.00.

#301 Master Dillinger, glass eyes, excellent plus condition, $450.00 – 550.00.

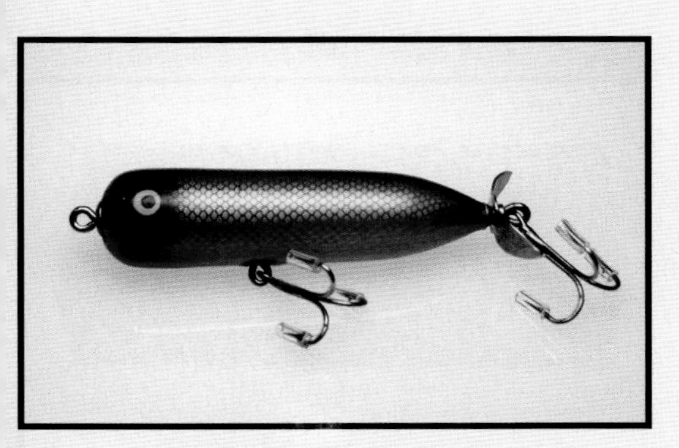

#815 Fuss-Budget, excellent plus condition, $90.00 – 100.00.

Two-piece cardboard box, "Victory," excellent condition, $50.00 – 75.00.

Michigan Lake Tackle Co., Grand Rapids, Michigan

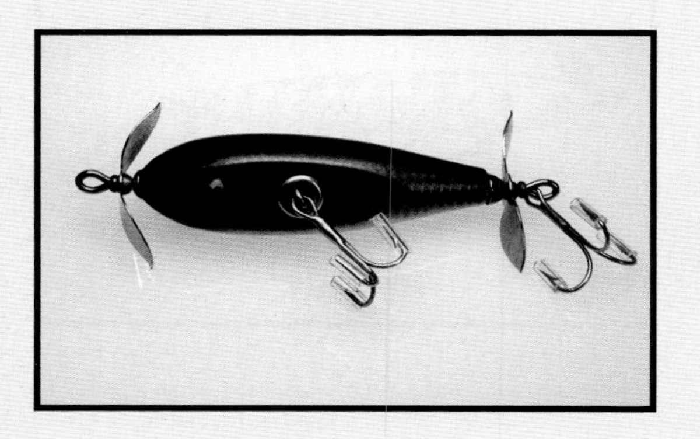

Fin-Wing, glass eyes, excellent plus condition, $60.00 – 80.00.

Fin-Wing two-piece cardboard box, excellent condition, $10.00 – 20.00.

Joe Froelich, Sayner, Wisconsin

J.F. Deep Runner, excellent condition, $65.00 – 75.00.

James Heddon's Sons, Dowagiac, Michigan

#2100 YRH Crazy Crawler, excellent condition, $40.00 – 50.00.

#9630 Punkinseed, plastic, excellent plus condition, $50.00 – 60.00.

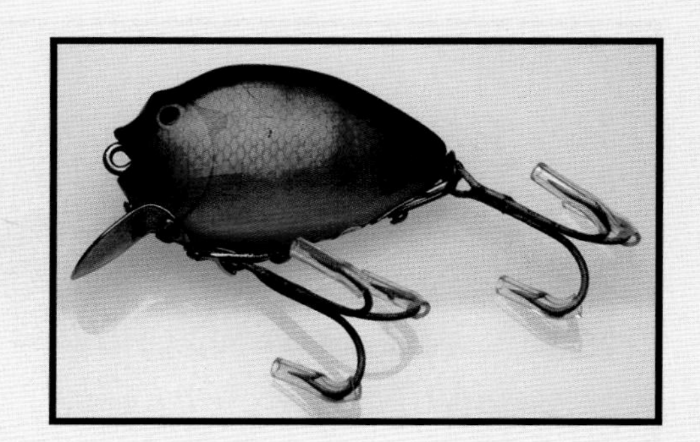

#730 BG1 Punkinseed, wood, excellent plus condition, $75.00 – 100.00.

Hoorocks-Ibbotson Co., Utica, New York

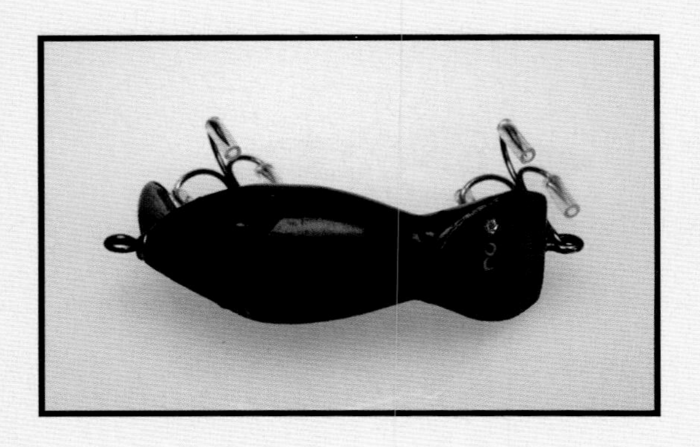

Krazy Kritter, black, excellent plus condition, $25.00 – 40.00.

Isle Royale Co., Jackson, Michigan

#8888 Eager Beaver, excellent plus condition, $25.00 – 35.00.

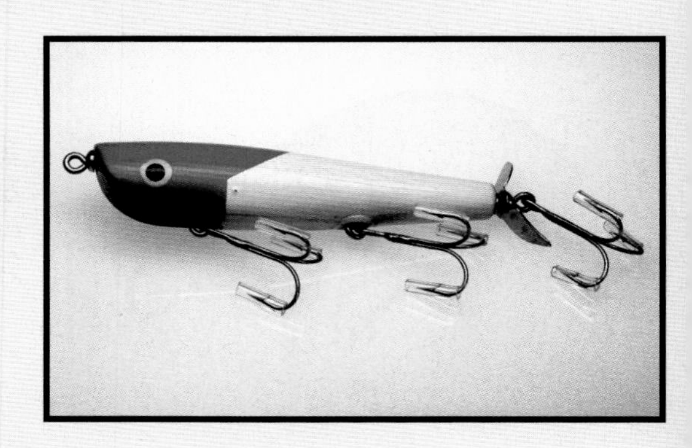

Two-piece cardboard box, excellent condition, $15.00 – 20.00.

W.J. Jamison Co., Chicago, Illinois

#1803 Wig-L-Twin, excellent condition, $30.00 – 40.00.

#1503 #1500 Series, plastic, slide-top cardboard box, excellent condition, $80.00 – 100.00.

Fred C. Keeling, Rockford, Illinois

Round-Body Expert, glass eyes, mottled finish, excellent condition, $800.00 – 1,000.00.

Little Tom, perch, excellent condition, $60.00 – 80.00.

Two-piece cardboard box, excellent condition, $90.00 – 120.00.

Oceanic Tackle Shop, Miami, Florida

#307 Leaping Lena, excellent plus condition, $30.00 – 40.00.

Two-piece cardboard box, excellent plus condition, $20.00 – 30.00.

Manning's Shrimp Wire Co., New Orleans, Louisiana

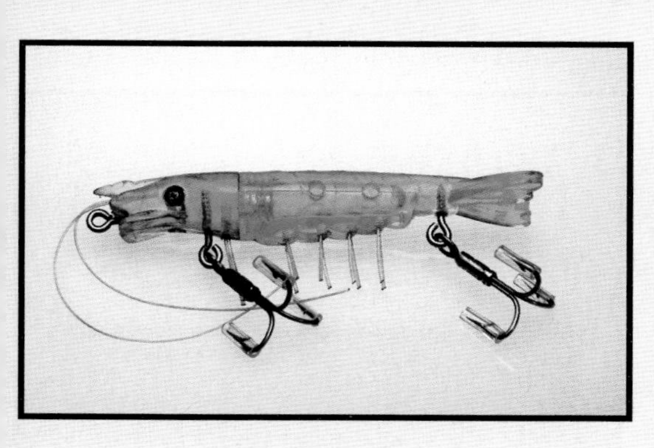

Manning's Tasty Shrimp, green, excellent plus condition, $35.00 – 50.00.

Cardboard box, excellent condition, $25.00 – 30.00.

Johnny Marsh Baits Inc., Daytona Beach, Florida

Marsh Marvel, excellent plus condition, $40.00 – 60.00.

Two-piece cardboard box, excellent plus condition, $40.00 – 60.00.

Moonlight Bait and Novelty Works, Paw Paw, Michigan

#907 Pikaroon Minnow, excellent plus condition, $1,000.00 – 1,500.00.

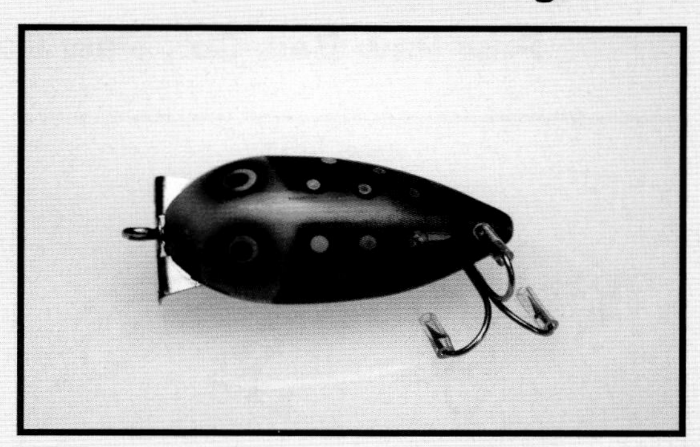

#1800 Ladybug Wiggler, excellent plus condition, $600.00 – 800.00.

Nichols Lure Co. Inc., Corpus Christi, Texas

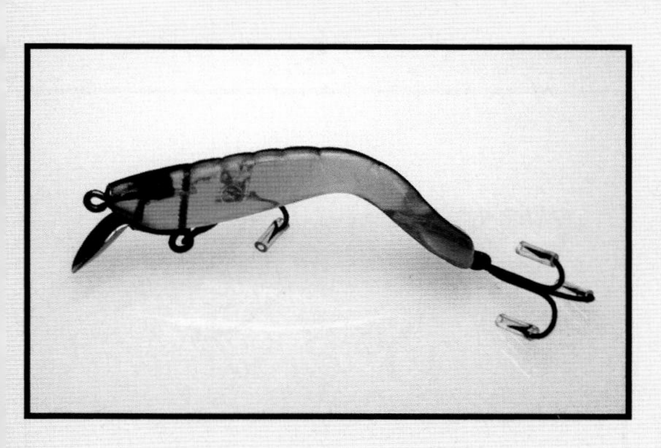

Shrimp, amber plastic, excellent condition, $60.00 – 75.00.

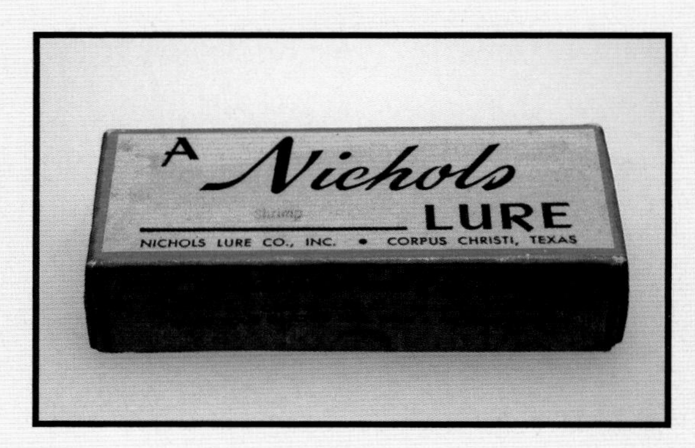

Two-piece cardboard box, excellent plus condition, $50.00 – 60.00.

Paw Paw Bait Co., Paw Paw, Michigan

#8555 Southern Swamp Minnow, bonehead finish, excellent plus condition, $90.00 – 120.00.

#5523 Plenty Sparkle, Dace, excellent plus condition, $80.00 – 110.00.

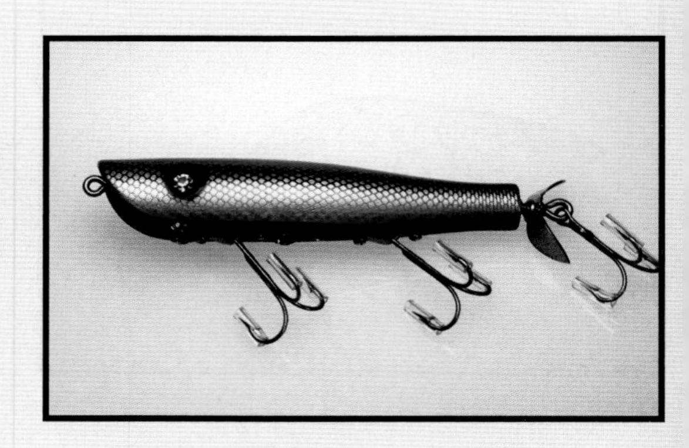

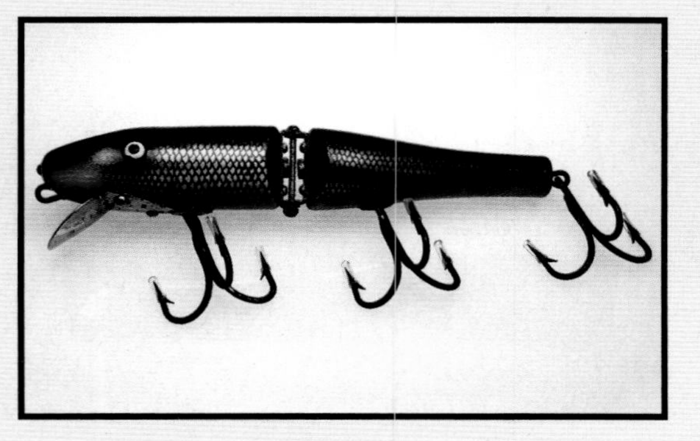

#05121-J Jointed Dreadnaught, chub, excellent condition, $175.00 – 250.00.

7800-1 Large Trout Caster, rainbow trout, excellent plus condition, $500.00 – 750.00.

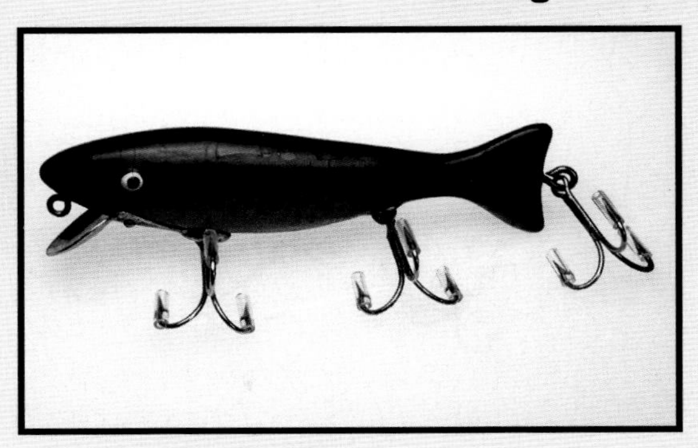

#924 River Type, brown trout, excellent plus condition, $100.00 – 125.00.

#3550 Small Bullhead, brown fur finish, excellent plus condition, $2,000.00 – 2,500.00.

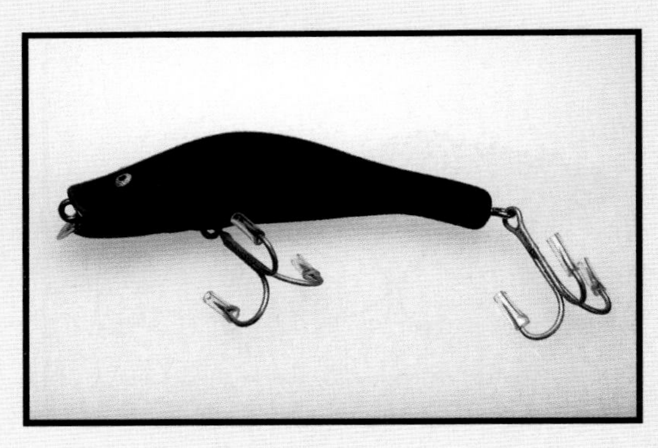

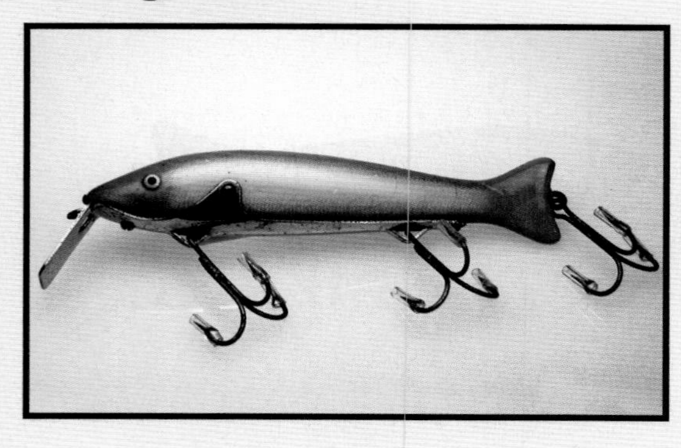

Spoon-Belly Wobbler, excellent condition, $800.00 – 1,000.00.

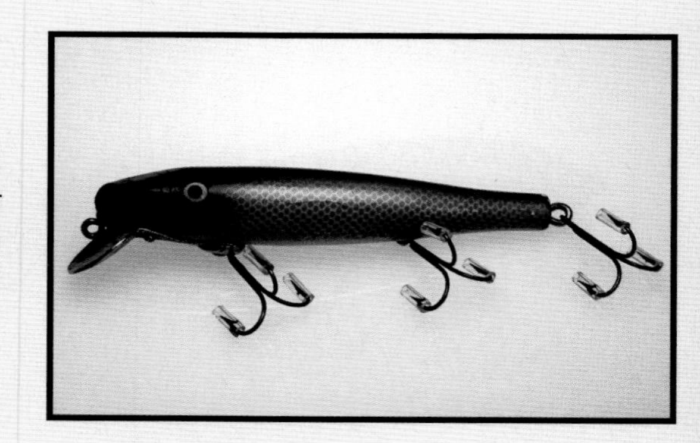

#1040 Piky-Getum, purple scale, excellent plus condition, $100.00 – 150.00.

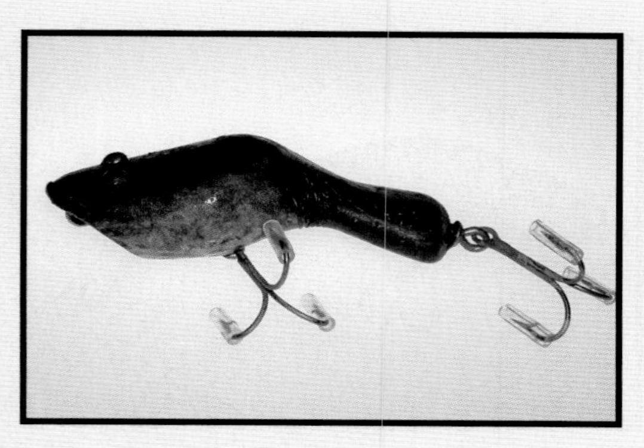

#71 Croaker Frog, frog skin, excellent plus condition, $75.00 – 125.00.

Jim Pfeffer, Orlando, Florida

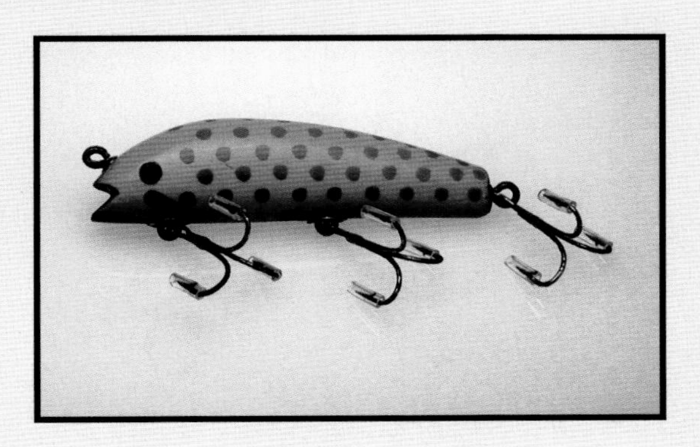

Banana Lure, yellow red dots, excellent plus condition, $225.00 – 275.00.

Orlando Shiner, silver shiner, excellent minus condition, $35.00 – 45.00.

Cast Top, red breast, excellent plus condition, $65.00 – 70.00.

Enterprise Manufacturing Co., Akron, Ohio

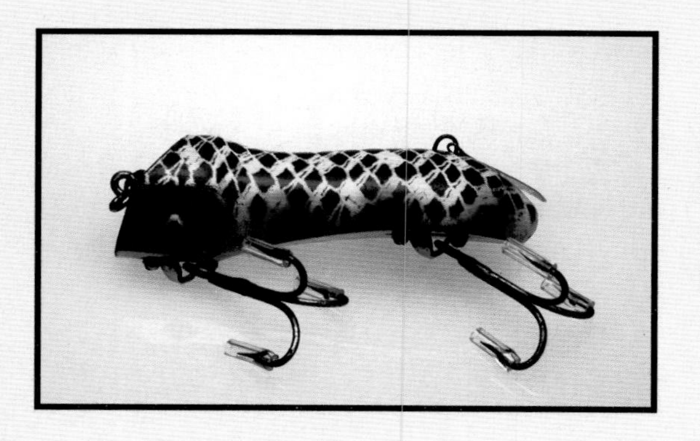

#4785 Wizard Wiggler, glass eyes, "Argyle," excellent minus condition, $300.00 – 350.00.

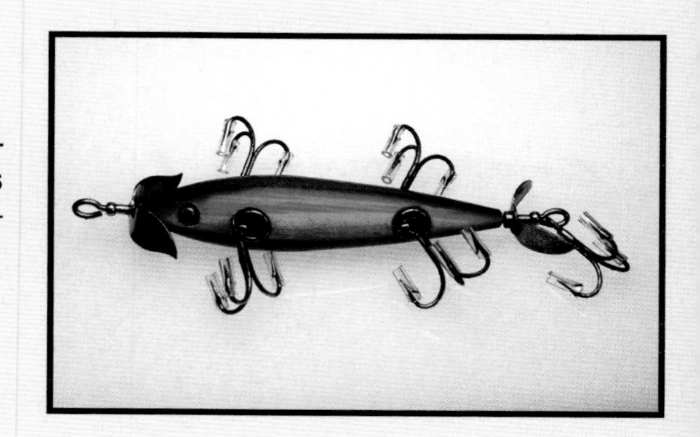

#3173 5-hook Neverfail Minnow, glass eyes, rainbow, excellent plus condition, $500.00 – 600.00.

Pflueger #5039 Pal-O-Mine, scramble finish, excellent plus condition, $75.00 – 125.00.

Pflueger #8400 Tantrum, black scale, excellent plus condition, $40.00 – 60.00.

Porter Bait Co., Daytona Beach, Florida

Two-piece cardboard box, cellophane window, excellent condition, $30.00 – 50.00.

S#15-21 Spindle, yellow perch, excellent plus condition, $60.00 – 75.00.

S#25-24 Dart-o, green back, pink side, silver scales, excellent plus condition, $??

S#35-11 Pop-Stop, grasshopper, excellent plus condition, $25.00 – 30.00.

U.S. Specialty Co., Syracuse, New York

Rush Tango, victory finish, excellent plus condition, $150.00 – 175.00.

Two-piece cardboard box, very good plus condition, $25.00 – 30.00.

The Shakespeare Co., Kalamazoo, Michigan

#6530 Little Joe, excellent plus condition, $100.00 – 150.00.

#6567 Jerkin' Lure, excellent plus condition, $75.00 – 100.00.

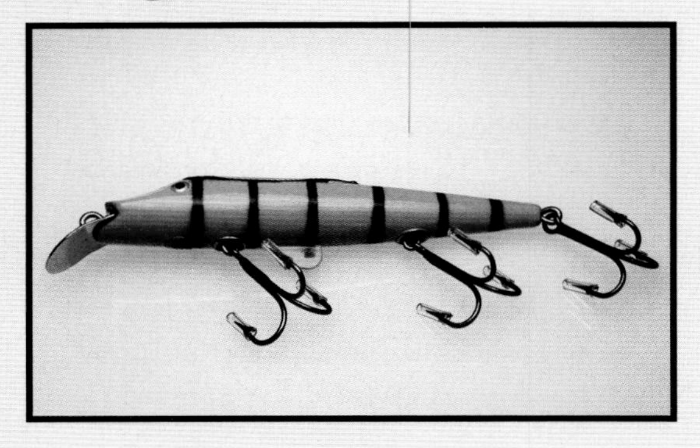

#6535 YJ Kingfish Wobbler, excellent plus condition, $150.00 – 165.00.

Creek Chub Bait Co., Garrett, Indiana

Shur-Strike BGM Baby Gar Minnow, Florida, special glass eyes, excellent plus condition, $225.00 – 300.00.

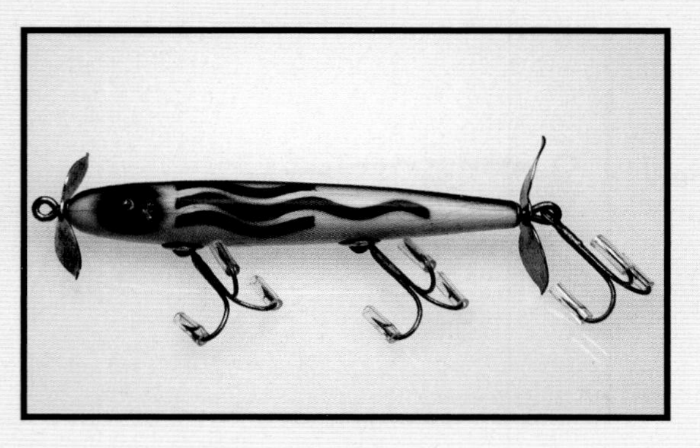

Shur-Strike GM Gar Minnow, Florida colors, painted tack eyes, excellent condition, $125.00 – 150.00.

Two-piece cardboard box, "NRA" stamped, excellent plus condition, $50.00 – 60.00.

Florida Artificial Bait Co., St. Augustine, Florida

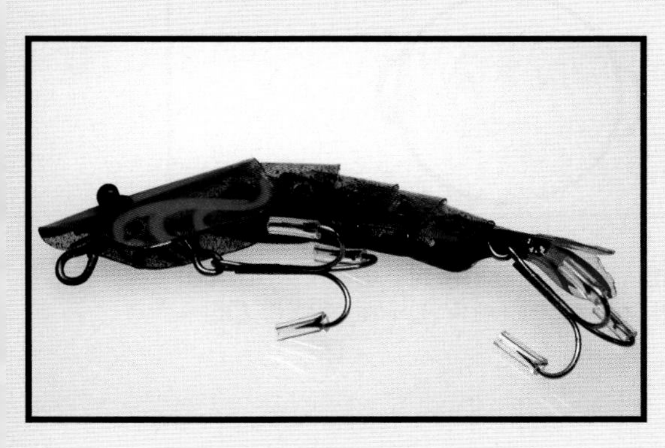

Superstrike Shrimp, excellent plus condition, $450.00 – 500.00.

Uncle Charlie Edwards, Orlando, Florida

Florida Banana, excellent plus condition, $50.00 – 60.00.

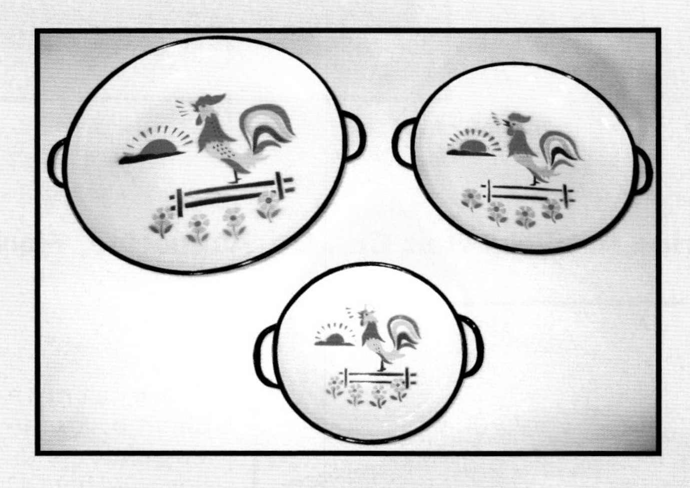

Three-piece set, white enamel with rooster scene, handled pans, black trim, $70.00 – 75.00 set.

The American graniteware industry was created out of necessity. After 1865 there were hundreds of factories and thousands of workers in the northern states who had produced military goods for General Grant's army in the Civil War. After the fighting was over and peace was restored to varying degrees, the industrial North needed something to manufacture and a growing population needed something to buy.

Graniteware was manufactured by dipping two or three coats of enamel over steel or iron base metals formed into utilitarian goods ranging form washboards, teapots, food molds, salt shakers, and dustpans to butter churns and bowl and pitcher sets.

Graniteware was durable, inexpensive, and utilitarian. It was produced to be used on a daily basis. If it was rusted, chipped, cracked, or discolored, it was easily replaced by the homemaker. It was popular from the 1870s into the 1930s. Graniteware was finally pushed out of American kitchens and pantrys by the rise of lighter and equally inexpensive aluminum products. The final blow was the beginning of World War II when steel and iron were dedicated to the war effort. Millions of pieces of graniteware ended up in local scrap drives to generate steel and iron for recycling into ships and cannons.

Graniteware has also been labeled: speckleware, agateware, enamelware, porcelainware, glazedware.

The first pieces were made in Europe in the late 1830s. Generally, the heavier the weight of the steel or cast iron under the enamel, the earlier the piece of graniteware. Cast iron handles can date the piece before 1900 and wooden handles often are found on pieces from the period before World War I (1900 – 1914). Look for pieces with seams, wooden knobs, tin lids, and pewter trim.

Among the more desired examples today are: advertising pieces, salesman's samples, miniatures made for children, butter churns, unused pieces with original paper labels, railroad ware for dining cars and galleys, salt and pepper shakers, cobalt blue pieces, dustpans, syrup jugs.

Among the primary colors were blue, cobalt blue, gray, green, brown, white, copper red, and the rarer mottled, marbled, and speckled varieties. Various shades of the primary colors were offered by the leading manufacturers.

There were dozens of companies cranking out graniteware. Three of the leading makers were LaLance and Grosjean of Woodhaven, N.Y., St. Louis Stamping, and Volbrath of Sheboygan, Wisconsin.

Graniteware

The primary considerations for collectors are condition, color, type of piece (spoon or churn), surface, weight, age, price, paper, label (rare), pewter trim, made in America, wood or tin knobs, lids, or trim.

Like most collectibles that were utilitarian and mass produced during the first half of the twentieth century, examples of graniteware can be found at a yard sale in Idaho or at Antique Week in New Hampshire. Graniteware was in daily use throughout America for almost 75 years but only a fraction has survived to be discovered in Idaho or New Hampshire today.

Unlike a "one of a kind" that is almost impossible to accurately price, graniteware has a reasonably established national price structure because there are few pieces that could be classed as "one of a kind." The phrase "one of a few" is more applicable.

Graniteware Chronology

1830s Manufactured in Europe.

1860s Introduced with mixed success into the United States.

1870s – early 1890s Graniteware was made with cast iron handles.

1876 The Philadelphia Exposition featured several exhibitors of graniteware and new interest among homemakers was sparked.

Early 1900s Graniteware was made with wooden handles.

1914 World War I forced numerous European makers to produce military goods rather then graniteware. Austrian and German manufacturers of graniteware were especially affected by the war.

1930s Production of aluminum household goods changed the buying patterns of American homemakers, and graniteware was no longer as popular; production significantly decreased.

The illustrations that follow are from the extensive inventory and collection of Central Illinois antiques and collectibles dealer Donna Vaughan. Ms. Vaughan can be reached by telephone at 309-724-8471.

Double-Boiler, red and cream three pieces, $40.00 – 45.00.
Teapot, red with black trim and wood handle, $60.00 – 70.00.

Mixing bowls, cream and green 6" & 7", $14.00 – 17.00 each.

Strainer, white with black trim, $18.00 – 22.00.
Strainer, white with red trim 8½", $15.00 – 20.00.
Strainer, white, with pan hook, $14.00 – 18.00.

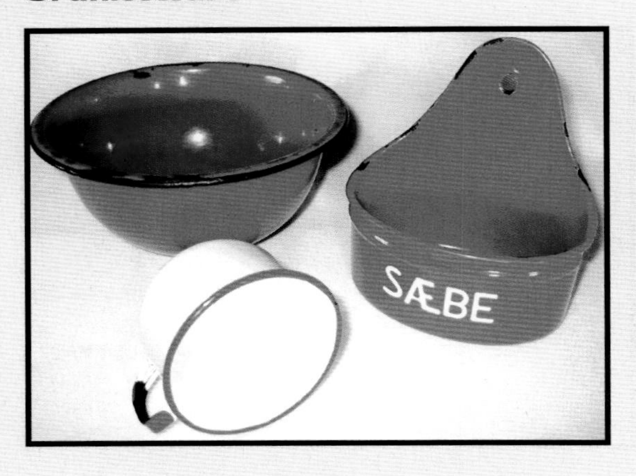

Bowl, red with black trim, 9", $20.00 – 24.00.
Handled cup with red trim & handle, $10.00 – 14.00.
Salt, red with white letters, Sweden, $65.00 – 70.00.

Dipper, red and green, unusual combination, $25.00 – 35.00.
12" bowl, black trim, $25.00 – 30.00.

Lid, red, 8", $5.00 – 8.00.
Pan, blue with white interior, small, $12.00 – 15.00.

Funnel, medium blue with white interior, $14.00 – 17.00.
Dipper, medium blue dipper with black handle, Yugoslavia, $15.00 – 18.00.

Coffeepot, powder blue and white, 11½", $60.00 – 65.00.
Bowl, large medium blue with black trim, large, 12", $25.00 – 28.00.

Roaster, cobalt blue, large, $40.00 – 48.00.

Cups and plates, orange trim, unusual color, $10.00 – 12.00 each.

Lidded diaper pail, white with red trim, $30.00 – 35.00.

German measure, white with cobalt trim, $30.00 – 36.00.
Pitcher, white with cobalt trim, $18.00 – 22.00.
Cup, small, white with cobalt and trim, $14.00 – 18.00.
Lidded pail, white with black trim, $30.00 – 38.00.

Chamber pot, shaded blue, early, $70.00 – 80.00.

Tea kettle, blue and white, large, $100.00 – 130.00.

Cup, black trim, with handle, $9.00 – 13.00. **Covered pot,** white lid, $20.00 – 28.00.

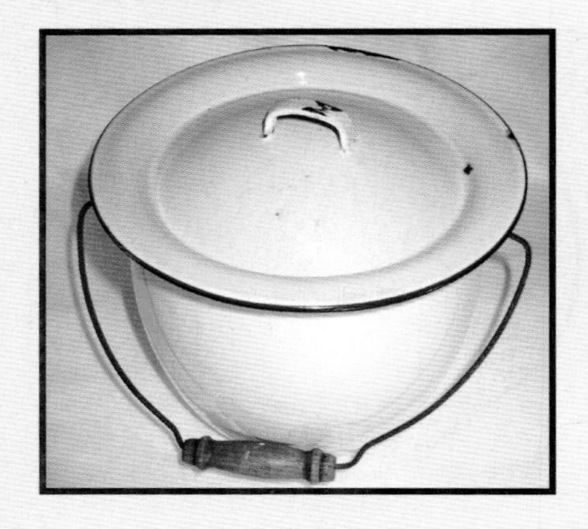

Milk can with lid, white with cobalt trim, $55.00 – 70.00.

Plates, cobalt rim, $8.00 – 10.00 each. **Pan,** $22.00.

Saute pan, large mottled gray, $28.00 – 32.00.

Pitcher with "drop" handle, red with white interior, $24.00 – 30.00. **Berry bucket,** brown and white spatter, $40.00 – 45.00.

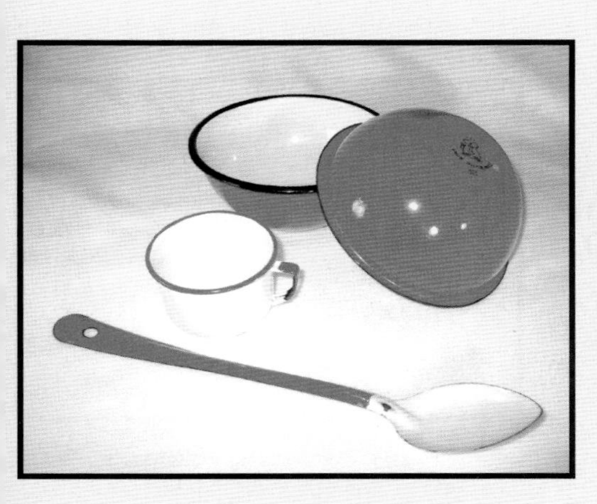

Sauce spoon, red and white, extra long 15", $20.00 – 24.00. **Bowls,** red with black trim and white interiors, Poland, $25.00 – 28.00 **Cup,** white with red trim and handle, $8.00 – 10.00.

Wash pan, cream and green, large, 18", $30.00 – 35.00. **Handled cup,** cream and green, $8.00 – 12.00. **Bowls,** $12.00 (each).

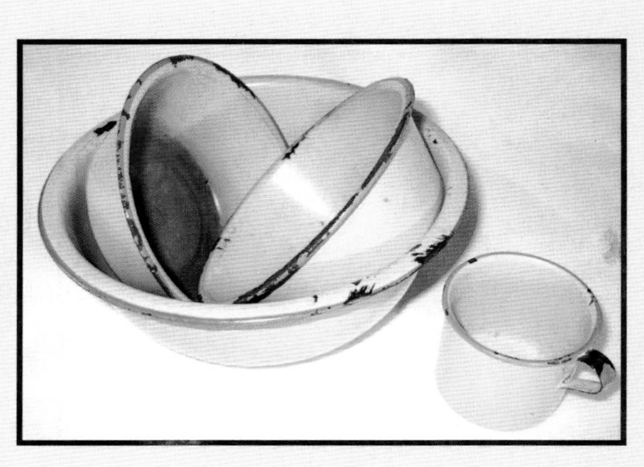

Pitcher, cream and green, large, 9½", $35.00 – 45.00.
Bowls, cream and green, 7", $6.00 – 9.00 each.

Wash pan, cream and green, large, 18", $30.00 – 35.00.

Bowl, red trim, large, 12", $14.00 – 17.00.
Bowl, green, $15.00 – 18.00.

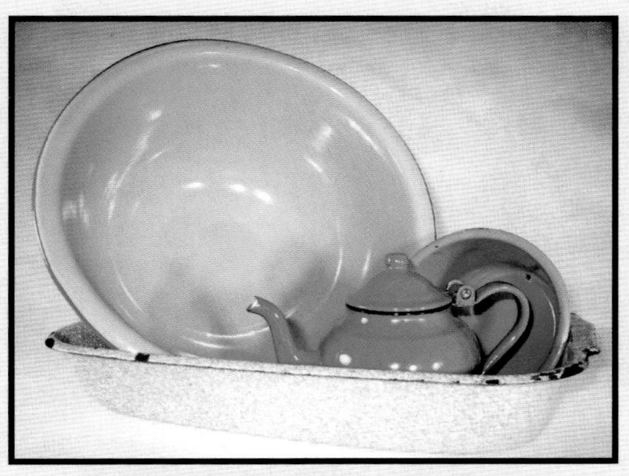

"One-cup" teapot, medium green, $18.00 – 22.00.
Pan, light green with medium green trim, large 12", $22.00 – 24.00.
Bowl, $12.00 – 14.00.

Marx Toys

Group of Marx toys.

The authors appreciate the assistance of Philip Edwards on this section. As is obvious from the photographs, Mr. Edwards is a very serious collector.

Mr. Edwards can be reached by e-mail at: pedwar@verizon.net.

There were several very excellent and well-known manufacturers of tin windup toys before World War II — Chein, Lehmann, Strauss, Marx, and others. The lithograph process was applied to thin sheets of tin to produce children's toys. During the 1930s, tin toys were mass produced which made them plentiful and cheap, thus rivaling the popularity of cast iron toys.

I do not remember much of the toys given to me as a 1930s child. I do remember rubber guns that I made to do battle and I had toy soldiers to simulate battle conditions. I also spent hours with skates, marbles, and yo-yos. My first bicycle provided the opportunity to range far and wide. Therefore, collecting 1930s windup toys is not a nostalgic recollection of childhood memories. It is, perhaps, the desire to have toys now that I did not have as a child.

I was attracted to tin windup toys while attending flea markets, garage sales, and antique shows in my quest for Boy Scout memorabilia. My first toy purchase was the Marx Merrymakers. I paid $150.00 for it. The toy was a mechanical marvel with bright colors and excellent construction. Later I learned that the toy sold for ninety-eight cents in 1931. Next I got a bargain for two Marx toys — Buck Rogers 20th Century Rocket Ship and the Flash Gordon Rocket Fighter — $200.00 for the pair. The bright, vivid colors, the mechanical ingenuity, and their excellent construction inspired me to look for other Marx toys and thus the desire to collect these fascinating toys exclusively.

Marx toy catalog with 47 pages showing the toys available to buyers (stores). The catalog was not distributed to the general public. $1,500.00.

Sand Ferris Wheel

PROPERTY OF
MARX TOYS, INC.
R. & D. DEPT.

Friction Racer and Bus

A page from the 1930 Marx catalog, "Property of Marx Toys, Inc. R & D. Depart."

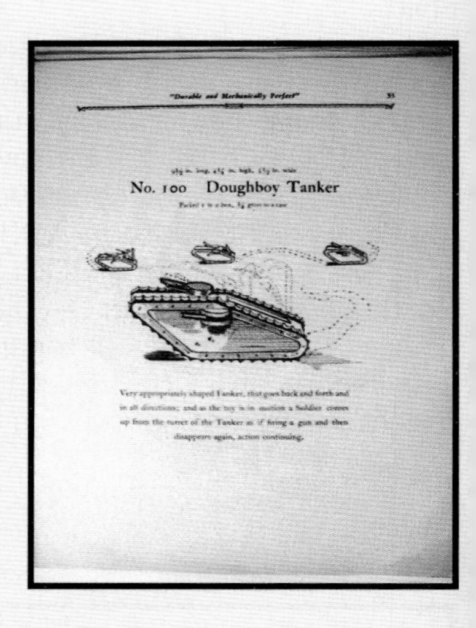
"Durable and Mechanically Perfect" 33

No. 100 Doughboy Tanker

Very appropriately shaped Tanker, that goes back and forth and in all directions; and as the toy is in motion a Soldier comes up from the turret of the Tanker as if firing a gun and then disappears again, action continuing.

Page 33 from the 1930 catalog, showing the No. 100 Doughboy Tanker.

Logo used from the early 1920s to February 1939 (first logo).

Logo used on Marx toys from February 14, 1939, to the end of the 1950s (second logo).

Sparkling Soldier Motorcycle, produced in c. 1940, described as a soldier and corporal, $500.00.

Police Siren Motorcycle, produced c. late 1930 and sold for $0.57, $350.00.

Motorcycle Delivery toy, five versions of this toy, the cart may or may not be perforated, $400.00.

Display of Marx airplanes.

New York Honeymoon Express, appeared in 1928, originally sold for $0.49, airplane often missing, $1,000.00 (toy); $200.00 (box).

City Airport, mid- to late 1930s, has beacon light housing missing, airplanes did not come with the Airport set, currently not known what aircraft, if any, were included in the set, $300.00.

Popeye the Pilot, appeared in 1936, earlier version has "47" on the side of the plane, later examples did not; the "47" adds about $200.00 to the toy. $1,100.00.

Rollover Plane, first appeared in 1947, also a red version, $400.00.

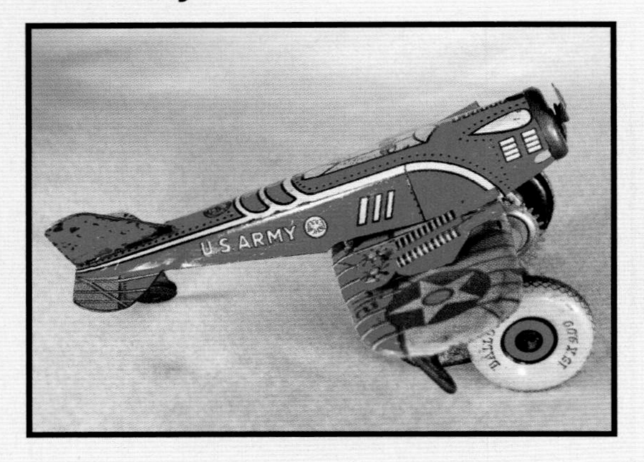

Pursuit Plane, first appeared in late 1930s, three versions exist, earliest has a cockpit tapped into the top of the fuselage, $250.00.

Pursuit Plane, army brown in color, $250.00.

Mail Plane, first appeared in 1936, $275.00.

Army Bomber, similar to the civilian mail plane in shape, appeared in 1938, $250.00.

Flash Gordon Rocket Fighter, appeared in 1939, Marx re-issued the toy in 1951 without Flash Gordon's name, $900.00.

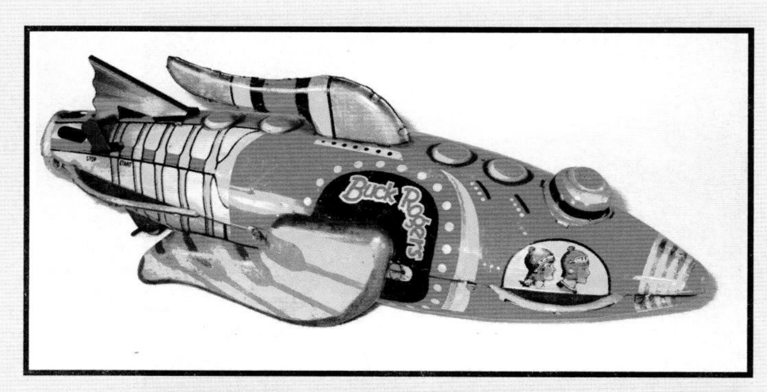

Buck Rogers 25th Century Rocket Ship, appeared in 1934, $900.00 (toy); $200.00 (box).

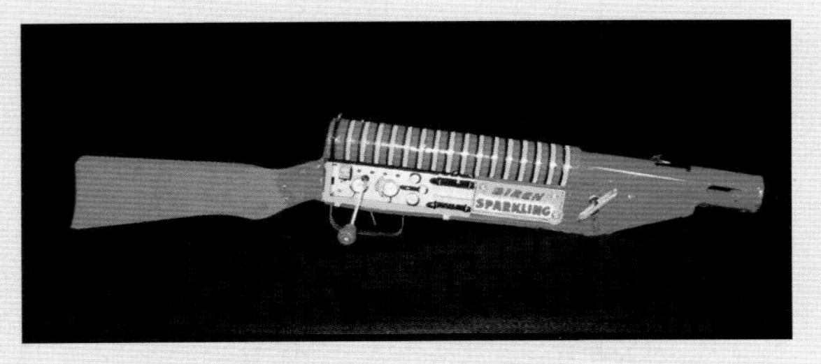

Siren Sparkling Machine Gun, appeared in 1947, $70.00.

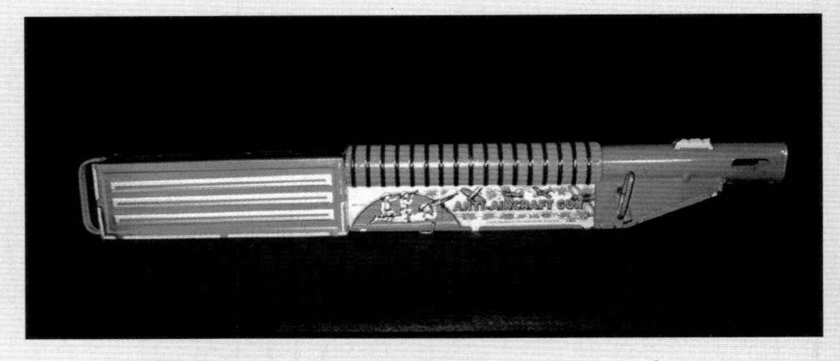

Anti-Aircraft Gun, appeared in 1941, $70.00.

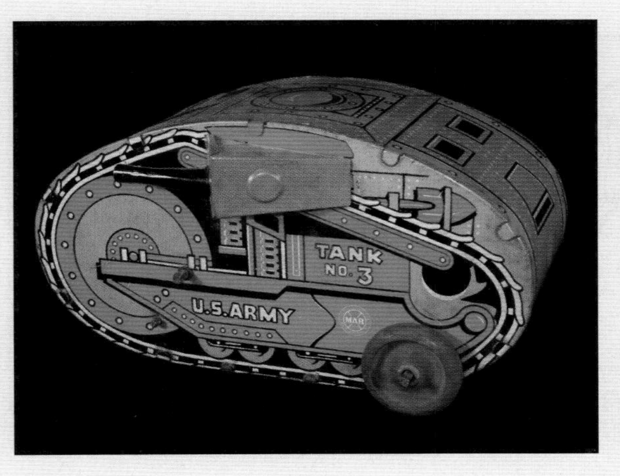

No. 3 Army Turnover Tank, this tank appeared in the late 1930s – early 1940s, there are a minimum of six versions of this toy, $200.00.

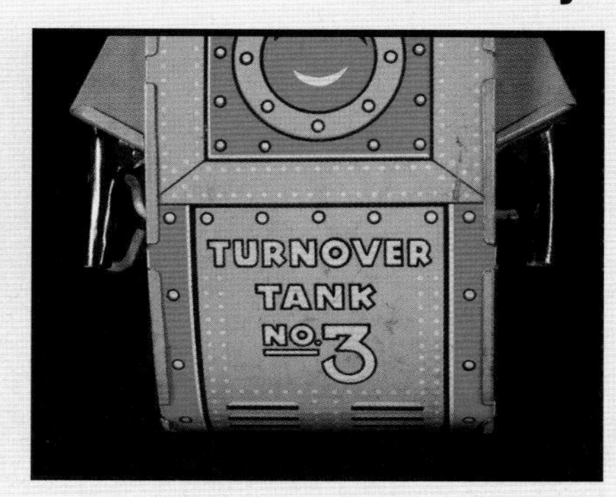

Front view of the No. 3 Army Turnover Tank.

Army Tank #12, appeared in the early 1940s, $250.00.

10" Doughboy Tank, appeared in the late 1930s – early 1940s, $300.00.

Side view of the soldier, note three cherons, red jacket, and World War I style hat.

U.S.S. Washington Battleship, first appeared in the late 1940s, box has title "Mechanical Sparkling Warship," $150.00 (toy).

Sparkling Soldier, crawls, appeared initially in 1935, $350.00.

Whoopee Cowboy Car, appeared in 1932, priced at $0.59, $700.00.

Cadillac Coupe, appeared in 1931, 11" long, a smaller version (8½") was offered at the same time, $500.00.

Army Truck, 10½" long, appeared in the 1930s, $450.00.

Toyland's Farm Products Milk Truck, rarely seen case and 12 bottles were included with the truck, offered in 1931, $400.00.

Mickey Mouse Locomotive, locomotive is 0-4-0, multicolored, windup. Box car is not pictured. $800.00 (includes entire set).

Mickey Mouse Gondola.

Mickey Mouse Train tender.

Mickey Mouse Caboose, #691521.

Charlie McCarthy in his Benzine Buggy, appeared in 1938, wooden hubcaps are standard although one version has metal hub-caps, originally sold for $0.49. $800.00 (toy); $200.00 (box).

Sheriff Sam and His Whoopee Car, appeared in 1949, catalog #744, priced at $0.94, $350.00.

Display of Marx windup toys.

Big Load Van Company Truck, appeared in 1928, $400.00.

Coca-Cola Truck, appeared c. 1954, shown are a two wheeler and six Coke trays, $400.00.

Rocker Racer, appeared in 1935, $450.00.

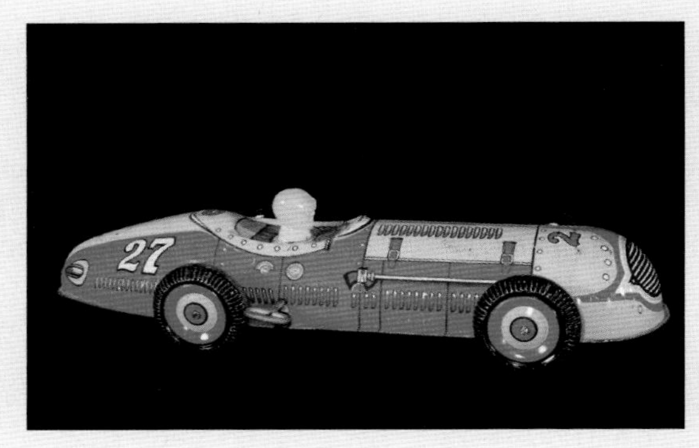

Mechanical Speed Racer, appeared in 1948, $300.00.

Range Rider, 10½" tall, c. 1940s, a smaller 8½" version was also made, $350.00.

Lone Ranger Target Game, appeared initially in 1938, $175.00 (includes gun and darts).

Gun with suction cup darts from the Lone Ranger Target Game.

American Tractor, appeared in 1926, $300.00.

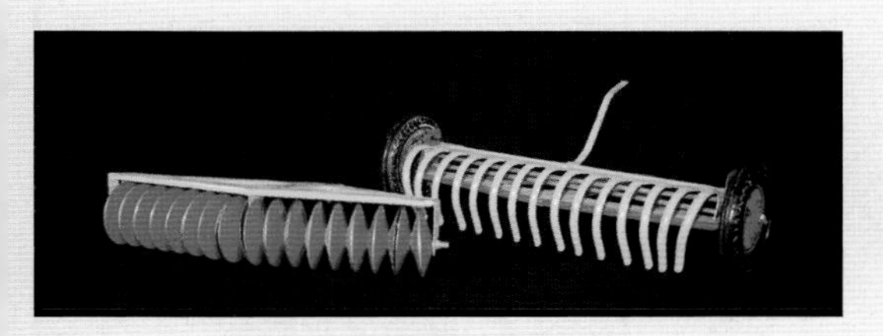

Tractor attachments, rake and disc, 1937, $40.00 (pair).

Road Roller with Driver, offered in 1930, $350.00.

Reversible Six Wheel Construction Tractor, offered in the 1960s, tools are included, $375.00.

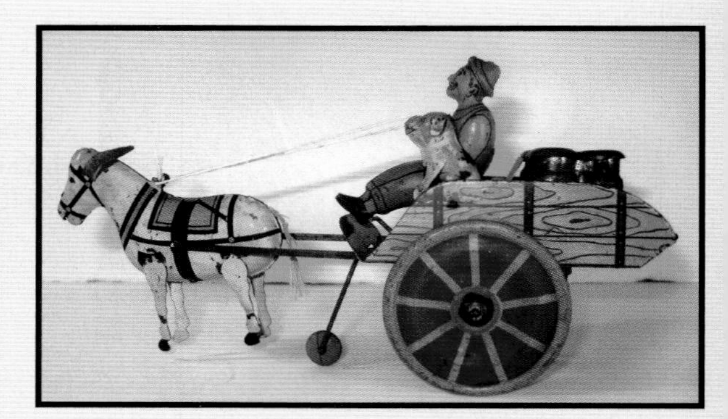

Hee-Haw Balky Mule, appeared in 1948, $510.00 (complete); $125.00 (without the milk cans and dog).

Milk Wagon and Horse, offered in 1931, later version had yellow wagon and "Grade A" logo, $400.00.

Amos 'n Andy Fresh Air Taxi, in 1938 Marx catalog, sold for $0.95. $1,100.00 (toy); $300.00 (box).

The slight rust on the under carriage and some wear is indicative of a genuine toy. A recent "fake" would typically not show either.

Be-Bop-The Jivin' Jigger, appeared in 1948, $400.00.

The box for the Jivin' Jigger, $100.00.

Charleston Trio, appeared in 1926, this example is a rarer version because the black dancer is the same figure found on the Marx Somstepa toy. The more commonly found example shows different colors for the clothes on the dancing figure.

Somstepa, first appeared in 1926, $750.00.

Dopey, first appeared in 1938, walker, $300.00 (toy); $100.00 (box).

Walking Pinocchio, appeared in 1939, has moving eyes, 1950s version has lithographed eyes, $470.00 (1939 version).

B.O. Plenty and Sparkle, appeared in late 1930s and early 1940s, $450.00 (toy); $65.00 (box).

Donald Duck Duet, appeared in 1946, $900.00 (toy); $200.00 (box).

Joe Penner and His Duck Goo Goo, appeared in 1934, sold for $4.15 per dozen, $600.00.

Little Orphan Annie Skipping Rope, appeared in 1931, sold for $0.25, $600.00.

Charlie McCarthy, walker, appeared in 1938, sold for $0.25, $350.00.

Popeye and Olive Oyl Jiggers, first appeared in 1937, $2,000.00 (toy); $500.00 (box).

Walking Popeye, first appeared in 1932, $550.00 (toy); $200.00 (box).

Popeye Express, produced in 1932, sold for $0.59, $500.00 (toy); $200.00 (box).

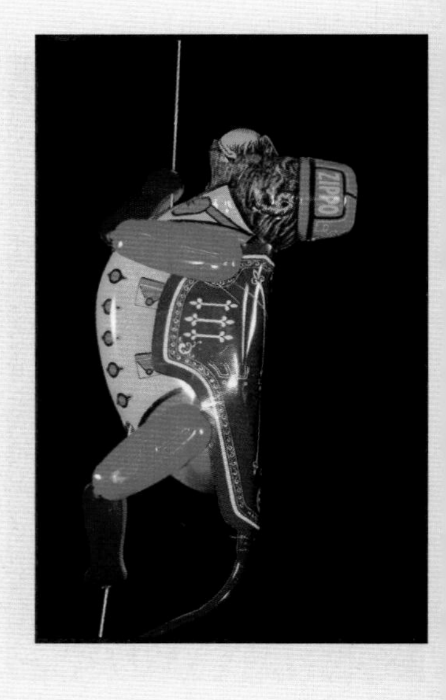

Zippo the Climbing Monkey, appeared in 1938, $175.00.

Tumbling Monkey on Two Chairs, offered in 1942, $200.00 (toy); $50.00 (box).

Mighty Kong, miniature version, appeared in the 1960s, wind-up toy, 8" tall. $375.00.
A battery-operated version is 11" tall and has a price tag of $600.00 – 700.00,

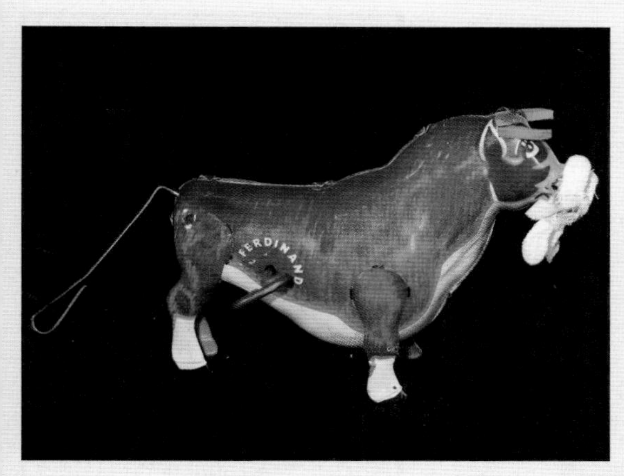

Ferdinand the Bull, appeared in 1938, cloth in the bull's mouth and the horns are often missing, $300.00.

Snappy the Miracle Dog, first appeared in 1931, $225.00.

Mid-Point Evaluation

We are approximately 50% through your learning experience and we need an instrument to measure your progress. Your participation in class and the quality of your demeanor have NOT been impressive to date.

The questions below will give us a completely subjective appraisal of your knowledge and should be taken very seriously.

Directions:
1. Read each question and select the most promising response.
2. Do not seek help from an outside source.
3. This is a timed and monitored exercise. The clock will be ticking and deviations from the norm will be reported.
4. Bellhops, vagabonds, and lawyers will be given a two-point bonus.
5. Begin.

1. The blue firkin or covered bucket is worth about $______.

2. True False The pestle is painted green.

3. This Odd Fellows ashtray is worth about $_____.

4. Willie Danials, a member of the Florida Highwaymen, painted this scene in the
a. 1920s
b. 1940s
c. after 1950
d. in the McLean County Jail
e. a & d

5. What is the approximate value (retail) of a collection of eight "hearts in hands?"

Mid-Point Evaluation

6. The factory-made "Housekeeper's Spice Box" is valued (retail) at about ______.

7. True False This William Tell mechanical bank dates from before the American Civil War.

8. In what state was the hickory arm chair made?

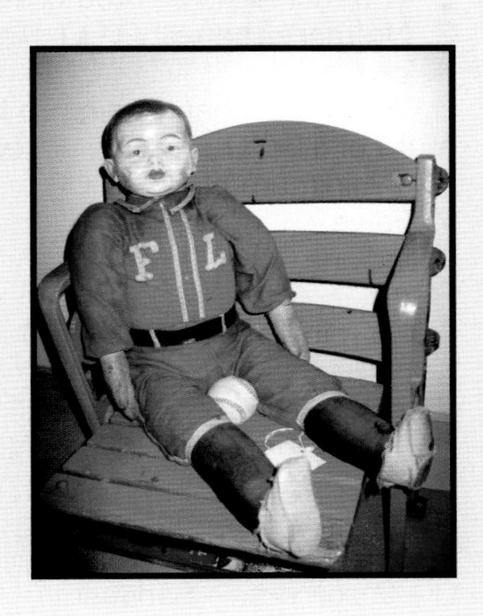

9. This doll in its original baseball suit dates from 1914 and was found in an attic in Utica, New York. The "F L" stands for
a. the Altoona Legends
b. the Fairhope Loons of the Florida State League
c. the Federal League
d. Frequent Freddy Love's All-Stars

10. The approximate value of the sign (tin on a wooden frame) is _____ (retail).

Mid-Point Evaluation

Answers

1. an absolute minimum of $350.00. Anything above that number is correct.
2. The mortar is painted green.
3. No more than $50.00. Anything under that amount is correct.
4. c
5. You are probably going to be surprised but anything above a minimum of $20,000.00 is acceptable.
6. a minimum of $200.00.
7. False
8. Indiana
9. c
10. a minimum of $300.00.

Scoring Scale

8 – 10 correct — Everybody down at the rendering plant will be so proud

5 – 7 correct — Sad

3 – 4 correct — Sadder

0 – 2 correct — Saddest

Felt Pennants

Emmit Wheeler and Karl Zehren of Odell, Illinois. They were enrolled at Illinois State Normal University in Normal, Illinois. The picture was taken during the 1914 – 1915 school year.

Karl, pictured at left, is *not* reading the original manuscript for this book and Emmit is *not* writing a ransom note for the daughter of the university president. Probably not.

Regardless, their room contains town, university, and literary organizations on felt pennants, and an I.S.N.U. football broadside from 1914. Most of their pennants would be priced in the $30.00 – 60.00 range today.

Early 1940s, strong demand, 8/10 rarity. The silk American flag is frayed a bit but it is an exceptional pennant that was probably sold at a post exchange on a military base during WWII. $150.00 – 160.00.

The Basics of Collecting Felt Pennants and Banners

The Basics of Collecting Felt Pennants and Banners

1. From about 1900 to the early 1950s, felt pennants with sewn-on letters decorated apartments, bedrooms, taverns, schools, dorm rooms, and other areas where students gathered.
2. Pennants were manufactured for academic organizations, Greek letter societies, high school and college graduating classes, specific events, the military, individual towns, tourist sites, national parks, sports teams, fairs, and colleges, high schools, and universities.
3. Pennants from professional sports teams with sewn-on letters actually are semi-rare and expensive. Most were printed. Football really did not blossom on a national scale until after 1950 so the earlier sewn pennants are in long demand and short supply.
4. Professional baseball teams offered pennants for sale at the ballparks in the early 1900s. Oddly, many of those pennants were stenciled or printed rather than offered with the sewn-on lettering. Pennants from before 1920, a World Series, the Federal League (1914 – 1915), and the various Negro League teams are especially rare and collectible.
5. Condition is a major issue in evaluating because the pennants were originally inexpensive, plentiful, subject to attack from moths, faded by the sun, hung by pins, tacks, or nails, and lightly valued by their owners. They were souvenirs.
6. The pre-1950 pennants that have survived are often found stored in trunks, attics, or piles in a basement. When the occupant of the room where the pennants were displayed left, graduated, or moved to the YMCA, the pennants were taken down and put away. The key to survival in a valuable form today is how they were stored. Pennants that have been refurbished, touched up to any degree, reshaped or trimmed, recolored, or repaired are significantly diminished in value.
7. Military units and post exchanges made available to trainees, cadets, and soldiers some spectacular pennants, wall pieces, table runners, and banners that are elaborately covered with sewn-on flags and decorative touches. The higher the level of patriotism during a period of time, the more detailed the felt pennant or banner.
8. There are rare factory-made table coverings of 10 – 18 pennants sewn together with examples from many colleges or states. There were factory-made felt bed coverings of specific colleges or university flags with a leather logo or crest with embossed lettering in the center. Generally, the blankets are sized for a single bed. These would be classed as "rare" and expensive ($200.00 – 400.00) if found with strong colors and in good condition.

9. For a pennant to have above average value it needs a combination of the following:
   a. leather patches
   b. flags or shields
   c. strong colors
   d. a lack of attention from moth or nail holes
   e. "sewn on" lettering
   f. no rips or problems or repairs
   g. an unusual subject matter, institution, or event
   h. a year or date
   i. original condition with no additions, repairs, or reshaping
10. Keep in mind the following:
   a. pennants and banners were usually produced in large numbers
   b. are seldom great works of art
   c. sold in bookstores and businesses shopped by students and tourists
   d. inexpensively made and sold
   e. often thrown away rather than repaired
11. They are *not* rare but they *are* becoming uncommon and prices are increasing each year. We feel that some of the best examples are still underpriced because many dealers are not aware of the pricing structure.
12. There are dealers who specialize in antique sporting goods and many of them offer a variety of pennants and felt banners among their merchandise. Generally these dealers are aware of the pricing patterns and mark their examples at full retail price. There are few bargains. On occasion a pennant or banner shows up in an unlikely location and the dealer has no ideas as to its real value. This might happen more often with felt pennants than exceptional furniture, advertising, or decorated stoneware because their values are more universally understood.
13. Ivy league, Big Ten, and eastern colleges and universities turn up on pennants, banners, and table/bureau runners from the 1920 to 1940s in much greater numbers than schools from the far west, southeast, or south.
14. The leather patches with collegiate names and seals usually date from the 1920s to 1930s and were embossed. An embossed leather patch addition to a pennant enhances the value about $15.00 – 20.00. A miniature silk American flag (usually a product of the years before or during WWII with 48 stars) adds about $20.00 – 25.00 to a pennant in at least excellent condition.

Condition Check-List

1. Fading caused by exposure to sun?
2. Cracking or missing paint in the silk screening?
3. Moth and insect damage?
4. Tip of the pennant intact?
5. Ribbons or tassels complete?
6. Have the colors "bled" or softened because of water or mold damage?
7. Pin or nail (tack) holes in the pennant?
8. Size of the pennant? (11" x 17" is a standard size)
9. Is the silk screening centered on the pennant?
10. Is the pennant a "re-print" of questionable age?

1957, little demand, 4/10 rarity, $8.00 – 10.00.

1980s, less than average demand, 3/10 rarity. It is unusual to find a pennant with a spelling error. Baseball related pennants that are older are much more in demand. This is a late gift shop pennant. $12.00 – 15.00.

1950s, little demand, 2/10 rarity, $8.00 – 10.00.

1940s, souvenir example, average demand, 3/10 rarity, $12.00 – 15.00 (still inexpensive).

1970s, little demand, 2/10 rarity, $8.00 – 10.00.

1950s, above average demand, 6/10 rarity. Table or bureau runners are not common. Will increase in value in short term as awareness grows. Good investment. $100.00 – 125.00.

1940s, souvenir collector, little demand, 3/10 rarity, letters are sewn-on, $14.00 – 16.00.

1980s, little demand, 1/10 rarity, $4.00 – 5.00.

1950s, moderate demand, 6/10 rarity. The dyed feathers add to the interest of the pennant and value, $20.00 – 25.00.

1958, little, if any demand (you had to be there), 2/10 rarity, $6.00 – 8.00.

1950, significant demand, 8/10 rarity. The Browns left St. Louis after the 1953 season, $100.00 – 120.00.

1980s, some demand, 3/10 rarity. A bowl game pennant should be dated (year as a minimum) and not generic. Undated pennants were brought out from the warehouse, the next time the Illini went to the Rose Bowl. Worth less than you would typically suppose, $8.00 – 10.00.

This is another generic pennant brought out of a warehouse when necessary, $8.00 – 10.00.

1950s, some demand, 6/10 rarity, sewn-on letters, $44.00 – 54.00.

1936, significant demand, 8/10 rarity. U.S. flag and sewn-on letters. Made for the 1936 Olympics in Berlin, Germany. $125.00 – 175.00.

1936, significant demand, 8/10 rarity. sewn-on letters and felt shield. Made in U.S. for 1936 Olympics. $125.00 – 140.00.

1920s, average demand, 5/10 rarity. Given the colors probably the U. of Nebraska. $35.00 – 40.00.

1915 – 1920, little demand, 3/10 rarity. Could be hundreds of high schools across 1920s America. $20.00 – 25.00.

1963, above average demand, 5/10 rarity. These unsold 1963 pennants were found in a warehouse in the 1980s. Had they been sold in 1963 not as many would have survived to be offered in perfect condition today. It would not be difficult to reprint pennants and have them mysteriously be found in a warehouse today. Always be concerned about provenance. $50.00 – 75.00.

1980s, some demand, 3/10 rarity. These are generic in origin and made to be sold at any point. A date would add much to the interest in the piece. This is another example of a "warehouse" find. $20.00 – 25.00.

1940s, limited demand, 4/10 rarity. More value in Peoria, Illinois, than any other place on the earth. $25.00 – 30.00.

1930s, average demand, 4/10 rarity, $20.00 – 30.00.

1950s, little demand, 2/10 rarity, $15.00 – 20.00.

1950s, above average demand, 6/10 rarity. The girl in the bathing suit makes this a little more interesting. $30.00 – 35.00.

1930s, above average demand, 6/10 rarity. The leather football patch is a plus. $40.00 – 50.00.

1940s, limited demand, 4/10 rarity. The Native American adds to the interest of the pennant. $25.00 – 30.00.

1940s, above average demand, 8/10 rarity. Banners are very collectible. This felt example with sewn-on letters is 2' x 3'. A date would add value. $100.00 – 120.00.

1950s, significant, 9/10 rarity. Though Grange played in the 1920s his pennant was sold at Illinois football games in the 1950s. Pennants of individual stars are rare. $150.00 – 200.00.

Close-up of Red Grange on felt pennant with silk screening.

1950, above average demand, 7/10 rarity. For a printed pennant this is a fairly elaborate example. The eagle makes it semi-special. This pennant was probably purchased at West Point. $55.00 – 65.00.

1940s, minimal demand, 2/10 rarity, $12.00 – 15.00.

1950s, moderate demand, 6/10 rarity, $20.00 – 25.00.

1950s, above average demand, 6/10 rarity, $25.00 – 28.00.

1940, significant demand, 8/10 rarity. Pennants with silk flags tend to be offered for sale during periods of growing patriotism and are not common. $125.00 – 140.00.

1950s, average demand generally, but higher to collectors of amusement park related memorabilia, 7/10 rarity, $20.00 – 25.00.

1906 – 1920, strong demand, 9/10 rarity. The damage costs the pennant about $50.00 – 75.00 in value. The early football player in uniform is rare. $125.00 – 150.00.

1930, minimal demand, 4/10 rarity, $15.00 – 20.00.

1940, average demand, 5/10 rarity. "Sewn-on" letters but missing fringe. $25.00 – 30.00.

1948, strong demand in New England, 7/10 rarity. Pennant purchased at Fenway in 1948 and missing fringe. Good period pennant but not a great one. Printed lettering. Condition makes it $65.00 – 75.00.

1950s, little, better than average demand, 6/10 rarity. Pennants from the deep South are not common. $25.00 – 30.00.

1910, minimal demand, 6/10 rarity. Loss of fringe and general condition hurts the pennant. $15.00 – 18.00.

1920, good demand, 6/10 rarity. Condition really hurts interest and value. We would pass on examples in this condition. $15.00 – 18.00.

1930s, below average demand, 6/10 rarity. Condition a potential problem. $20.00 – 30.00.

1930s, good demand, 6/10 rarity. Another example of a pennant from the South adding to value. $20.00 – 25.00.

This is an example of an embossed (impressed) university seal on a felt pennant with sewn-on letters from about 1940. The leather circular seal adds about $15.00 – 20.00 to the total value of a pennant assuming everything else is in at least excellent condition. A leather embossed seal will not make a bad pennant automatically into a more desirable one. Condition is still absolutely essential in the evaluation process of any pennant or banner made of felt.

1917, strong demand, 9/10 rarity. This is an exceptionally detailed pennant from 1917. The fringe on the "7" adds a touch. $150.00 – 175.00.

Chicago Cubs 1984 league championship pennant, probably strong demand and getting stronger, 7/10 rarity. This is a phantom pennant because San Diego was the National League champion. Technically these might not have been sold and were printed in anticipation of victory but Leon Durham got in the way. $50.00 and will increase.

1920 – early 1940s, strong demand, 8/10 rarity. The pillow covers are found with military, college, and university decoration and logos. We have not seen covers with professional teams displayed. $135.00 – 160.00.

The "DJR" class of 1932 with the block M was decorated by an amateur seamstress after the pillow cover was purchased. Again, western, southern, and southeastern colleges do not show up as often as eastern and midwestern schools on the covers. This would also fall in the $135.00 – 160.00 price range.

Schoenhut Circus Toys

Schoenhut Circus.

Schoenhut circus performers and animals are typically evaluated on a five-point scale ranging from poor to mint. For our purposes we will assume that the animals and performers are in very good to almost excellent condition. This would indicate strong original paint, no repairs of consequence, and body parts intact. The clothing should also be original but a random moth hole is acceptable. The toys in this condition show signs of wear because they were played with but not abused. A quality job of restringing is *not* a negative in the evaluative process.

Reproductions of Schoenhut

As you already understand, a reproduction is designed to replicate and celebrate an earlier version of an object. A fake is a deliberate attempt to fool a buyer into purchasing an item that is misrepresented. From 1948 to about 1950 Harry Delavan produced a circus set (with rights obtained from the Schoenhut estate) that mimicked the Humpty Dumpty circus set. This was a reproduction manufactured in "the style of" the original set. About 1976 the B. Shackman Company of New York City created and briefly marketed a second similar set. The Shackman set was made in Taiwan.

Basics of Collecting Schoenhut Circus Toys

1. Statistically in your lifetime you are not going to travel to a farm auction, flea market, tag sale, or garage sale and find a Schoenhut wolf, rabbit, hyena, cat, or gorilla. You are infinitely more likely to discover a clown, donkey, or elephant with relatively little effort.
2. The Humpty-Dumpty circus was first made in 1903 by Schoenhut in Philadelphia. The company slowly closed down from 1935 to 1937 in the middle of the Great Depression when toys were not too high on many lists of essentials.
3. Animals with glass eyes date from prior to 1919 and are more desirable to collectors.
4. A reduced series of circus performers (5) and animals (16 plus a brown or white horse) was introduced in 1923. The reduced performers or personnel were about 6" in height as opposed to the 8" standard size.
5. A tent was offered for sale initially in 1906.
6. There are at least 20 different clown costumes and about 12 variations in the way the clowns are put together.
7. The hyena, zebra, gazelle, and gorilla were introduced with the Teddy Roosevelt Safari set (made from 1909 to 1912). The gorilla was only made with painted eyes.
8. The glass-eyed cat, rabbit, and wolf initially were part of the 1908 Farmer and Milkmaid set.

9. The two-part heads on the performers also date before 1919. They consist of a cast plaster face on a turned wooden head. There is a seam where the face was applied in front of the ears.
10. From a desirability standpoint, two-part heads are superior to the bisque and later one-part heads.

Retail Price Guide to Schoenhut Animals

Animal	Painted Eyes	Glass Eyes	Reduced Size
alligator	$575.00	$850.00	
brown bear	$700.00	$925.00	$675.00
buffalo	$750.00	$1,000.00	$825.00
bulldog	$1,000.00	$1,800.00	$650.00
burro	$625.00	$900.00	
Arabian camel (one hump)	$700.00	$875.00	
Bactrian camel	$700.00	$1,850.00	
cat	$2,800.00	$5,000.00	
cow	$725.00	$1,000.00	
deer	$850.00	$1,200.00	
donkey	$175.00	$250.00	$140.00
elephant	$175.00	$300.00	$150.00
gazelle	$1,500.00	$3,000.00	
giraffe	$700.00	$900.00	$600.00
goose	$800.00		
gorilla	$3,500.00		
hippopotamus	$575.00	$850.00	$500.00
dark horse	$400.00	$675.00	$400.00
white horse	$400.00	$675.00	$400.00
hyena	$2,500.00	$5,000.00	
kangaroo	$1,200.00	$1,800.00	
leopard	$700.00	$875.00	$600.00
lion	$700.00	$950.00	$600.00
monkey	$850.00		
ostrich	$750.00	$1,000.00	$600.00
pig	$575.00	$750.00	$900.00
polar bear	$1,275.00	$2,400.00	
poodle	$450.00	$875.00	
rabbit	$1,800.00	$5,000.00	
rhinoceros	$650.00	$1,000.00	$700.00
sea lion	$875.00	$1,200.00	
sheep	$800.00	$1,100.00	
tiger	$700.00	$1,000.00	$675.00
wolf	$2,000.00	$5,000.00	
zebra	$625.00	$1,000.00	$750.00
zebu	$2,200.00	$1,000.00	

Note: Prices for the glass-eyed poodle, lion, and buffalo refer to the cloth-maned style.

Retail Price Guide to Shoenhut Performers & Personnel

The prices of personnel/performers refer to the later, one-part head pieces. The earlier two-part heads and bisque heads are typically more expensive.

There were nine personnel/performers with the standard size and five with the reduced size.

	8" standard size	6" reduced size
Chinaman	$800.00	
clown	$250.00	$200.00
gent acrobat	$1,500.00	
hobo	$800.00	$650.00
lady acrobat	$675.00	
lady rider	$600.00	$450.00
lion tamer	$750.00	
black dude	$850.00	$700.00
ringmaster	$600.00	$450.00

Retail Price guide to Selected Circus Accessories

accessory	value
ball	$60.00
barrel	$35.00
bottle with label	$325.00
chair	$35.00
goblet	$25.00
ladder	$25.00
medium pedestal	$100.00
tall pedestal	$125.00
table	$65.00
teeter totter	$600.00
50 pound weight	$400.00
100 pound weight	$500.00
200 pound weight	$400.00
whip	$125.00

Note: All accessories are assumed to be in very good to excellent condition with minor wear.

Two Chinese acrobats.

Lady acrobat with one-part head.

Comic figure Moritz and a donkey from the "dollar set" that dates from the early 1930s. A complete "dollar set" consisted of a boxed miniature clown, elephant, and donkey with painted eyes.

Glass-eye alligators with leather feet.

Sea lion or seal with leather flippers, ball, and pedestal.

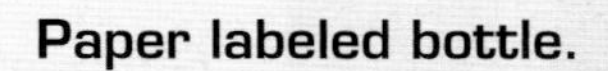

Paper labeled bottle.

200-pound weights for the gent acrobat/strongman.

Glass-eyed elephants with head pieces and blankets (howdahs).

Glass-eyed giraffes and their closed mouths.

Lion with glass eyes and cloth mane.

Dark face monkey with shorter legs than the taller white faced monkey.

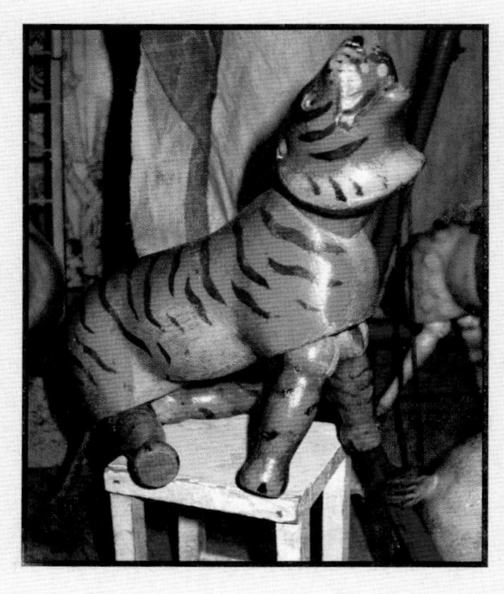

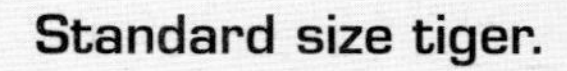

Standard size tiger.

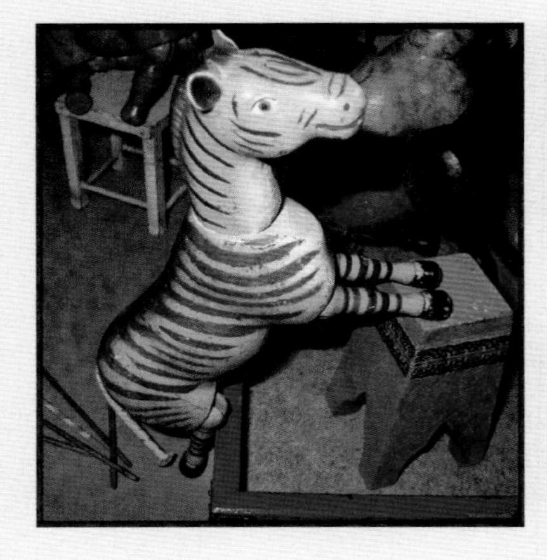

Painted-eye zebra with closed-mouth and one-part head and neck.

The most common animal is the donkey. This example has glass eyes and a blanket.

Tall pedestal.

Tub.

Barrel.

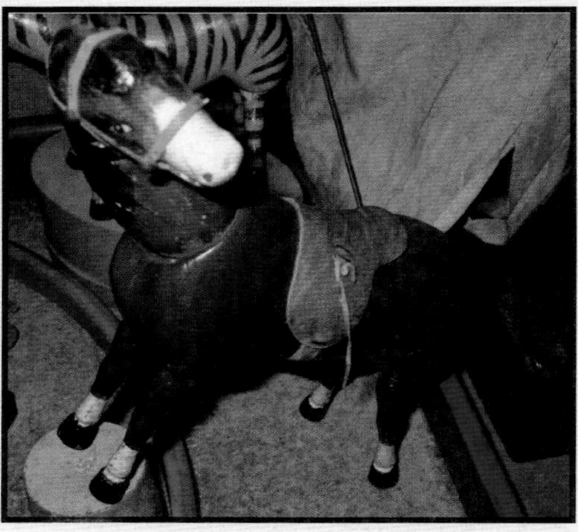

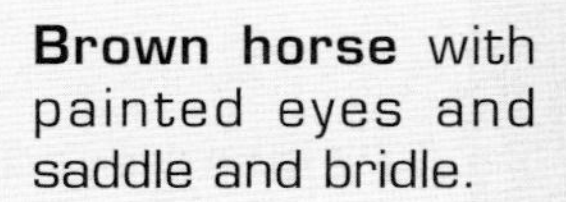

Brown horse with painted eyes and saddle and bridle.

Cage wagon from the early 1930s.

Glass eye rhino.

Painted-eyed and glass-eyed pigs.

Clown and barrel.

Two clowns and a tub.

Clown and pedestal.

Lion tamer with one-part head.

Gent acrobat/strongman with bisque head.

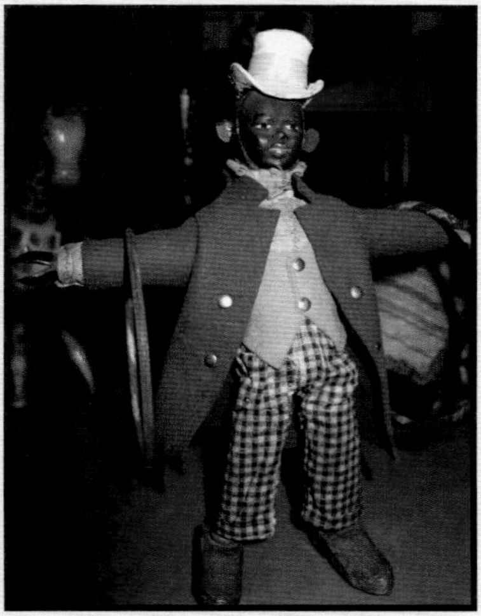

Black dude.

Stone Fruit

Stone Fruit

To include stone (marble) fruits and vegetables in a book about Americana is a semi-serious stretch because it's historically been sculpted in Italy by local artisans since Queen Victoria decided too much of anything is vastly superior to too little of something. We have bought stone fruit and vegetables in Cortona, Florence, and Rome in Italy and have made purchases at antiques markets in Paris, France; York, Pennsylvania; and 50 points and shows in between.

The quality of everything we purchased was fairly comparable and the prices paid were similar in all the geographic regions for old stone fruit and vegetables. There are rare pieces that can be priced at $1,500.00 and marble walnuts and strawberries at $25.00 – 40.00. The primary question is always the *age* of the produce.

In November of 2002 we saw a spectacular marble cantaloupe in York that was almost 14" in diameter and tagged at $1,400.00. The color was correctly faded to some degree and it looked old to us. We emotionally wanted to write the check but there was a lingering question that troubled us. Something was amiss.

Serious collectors who are specialists in a very thin slice of a huge antiques and collectibles pie contend that their initial glance, glare, focus, flash, vision, or look at a particular item is enough. They "know" whether it is "right" or "wrong" instantly, immediately in a flood of insight. Always.

If it instinctively comes up "right," they begin the buying process. If it comes up "wrong," they walk away and reconvene the hunt in the next booth.

Over time a collector sees hundreds (or thousands) of examples of whatever they collect. Each encounter provides a bit of information that is unconsciously filtered into a subconscious storage area that can be tapped when a need arises.

Stone produce, unlike a painted table, can't be turned upside down and inspected for shadows, repair, and secondary construction techniques. To recoin a phrase that you have heard somewhere before, it is what it is.

A week after the cantaloupe encounter in York we were in a shop in Pensacola, Florida, that, among many great things new and older, had an assortment of marble (stone) fruits and vegetables. There was a marble cantaloupe that was about 14" in diameter and priced at $45.00. The color was strong and the piece was added to our collection. The owners of the shop had found the contemporary stone fruit on a buying trip to Italy.

Notes:

1. Examples made a century apart are similar in color and technique. There have been few changes. The grandchildren are using the same grade of marble, coloring agents, and tools put down by their great-grandparents when they retired.
2. Oversized pieces, half pieces, and miniature examples of fruits and vegetables are less often encountered by collectors.
3. The only real difference between the "old" and the "new" is 50 – 100 years of exposure to sunlight, skin oils, bumps, drops, and dust.
4. In the 1870 – 1910 period of Italian immigration marble produce arrived in cardboard suitcases and potato sacks. It was inexpensive decorative "art."
5. Century old stone fruit tends to show up occasionally at tag sales in Italian enclaves in urban settings. It was a decorative staple in wooden bowls on mahogany veneered dining tables for four generations.
6. The surface of a piece of marble is altered over time naturally by exposure to light, dust, temperature, and contact with hands. It's difficult to fake.
7. The contemporary pieces in Italian shops are sold as contemporary pieces in the $18.00 – 35.00 range. When the stone produce reaches the United States and passes through four or five hands on the secondary market, things can change.
8. Condition is critical. Cracks, chips, and blemishes dramatically diminish the value of old and new pieces.
9. American servicemen from two wars have brought home thousands of pieces because they were available, representative of Italy, and were probably not going to break in transit. Tourists have been fueling the stone fruit and vegetable market for more than a century.
10. "Old" stone fruit really does have a patina or surface that you can consistently recognize if you have seen enough. Trust that unconscious ability that lurks beneath the surface and act on your first impression.
11. Much like decorated stoneware, a piece of stone fruit can take a minor problem or chip and maintain value if it is unique or extremely rare.

Stone Fruit

Three cherries with wire stems, probably contemporary, $25.00 – 30.00.

Two cherries, 1920s, the stems have been obviously replaced, $45.00 – 55.00 (pair).

Rare peach with carved marble pit, 1880 – 1910, a very early piece of fruit made from a single piece of marble, $1,500.00 – 1,800.00.

Pomegranate with stem, contemporary, $30.00 – 35.00.

Pomegranate, 1880 – 1910, $350.00 – 425.00.

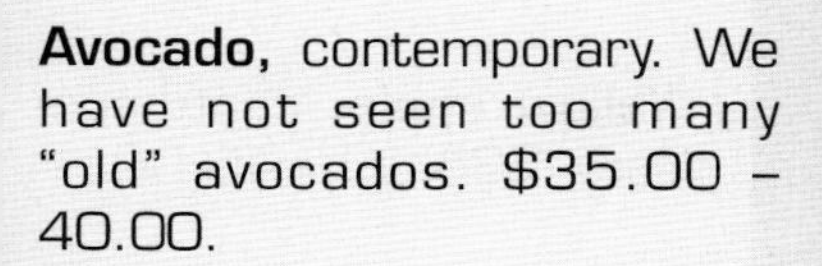

Avocado, contemporary. We have not seen too many "old" avocados. $35.00 – 40.00.

Fig, probably 1940, $75.00 – 85.00.

Yellow apple, contemporary, $35.00 – 40.00.

Yellow apple, contemporary, $35.00 – 40.00.

Red apple, contemporary, $25.00 – 30.00.

Half apple, 1930, $475.00 – 600.00.

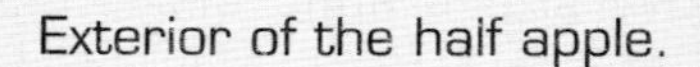

Exterior of the half apple.

Pomegranate, contemporary, $30.00 – 35.00.

Orange, 1930, $90.00 – 100.00.

Oversize orange slice, 7½", 1900 – 1920, $600.00 – 700.00.

Pear, contemporary, $45.00 – 55.00.

Peach, 1900, $65.00 – 75.00.

Half peach, 1890 – 1920, rare form, $500.00 – 575.00,

Peach, 1900 – 1920, $60.00 – 75.00.

Pear, contemporary, $30.00 – 40.00.

Red pear, contemporary (sadly). If there is a wooden stem and the piece is alleged to be original and complete, look at the stem. Wood darkens and shrinks over time as it dries out. $45.00 – 55.00.

Oversized pear, 8", 1900 – 1920, rare form and size. $400.00 – 500.00.

One-half pear 7", 1900 – 1920, $500.00 – 650.00.

Great peach, contemporary, $40.00 – 45.00.

Three bananas, 1890 – 1940, $65.00 – 75.00 each.

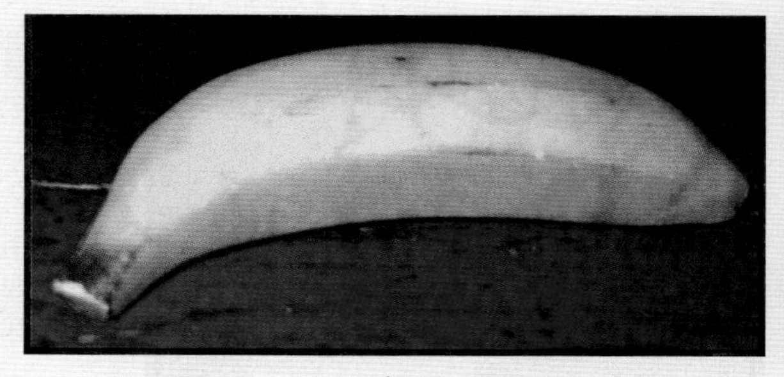

Banana, 1940, $65.00 – 75.00.

One of a pair of bookends with a pear and four pieces of miniature fruit, 1930s – 1940s. A miniature half pear is rare and the bookends, though not terribly old, are uncommon. Miniature fruit is also much rarer than conventionally sized examples. $500.00 – 600.00 pair.

Three walnuts, contemporary, $20.00 – 25.00 each.

Half orange slice, 1940, $400.00 – 475.00.

Orange, contemporary, $40.00 – 45.00.

Orange, 1940s, $65.00 – 75.00.

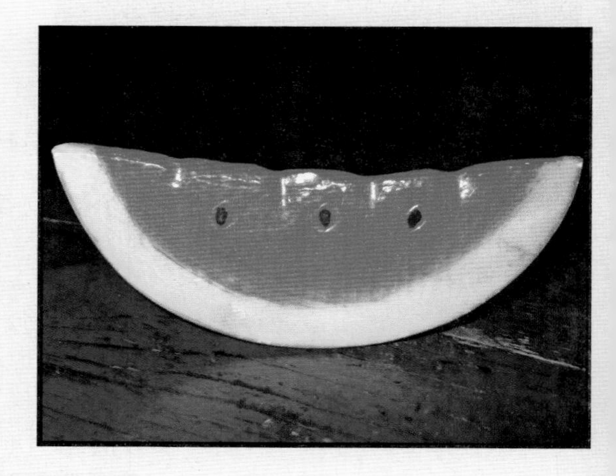

Watermelon slice, 1930 – 1940s. This is a really rare and valuable form. $700.00 – 1,000.00.

Three strawberries, 1940s, $50.00 – 55.00 each.

Cantaloupe, 1930s. Compare this example to the contemporary cantaloupe and you should see the differences. This piece, like most stone fruit, is lifesize. $1,000.00+.

Cantaloupe, contemporary. We do not see many lifesize cantaloupes or melons (new or old) for sale. $45.00 – 55.00.

Bowl of miniature stone fruit, 1930s – 1940, $40.00 – 45.00 each; $750.00 collection.

Pair of half lemons, rare, 1940s – 1950, $500.00 – 575.00.

Rare avocado pear half, 8", 1920, $1,000.00.

Interior of the avocado pear.

Bunch of grapes with stem, 1930s, $100.00.

Bunch of white grapes with stem, 1930s, $100.00.

Bunch of grapes with thick stem, 1930s, $100.00.

Persimmons with twig, contemporary, $30.00 – 35.00.

Pitcher, Burger and Lang, New York, cobalt flower, late third quarter nineteenth century, $800.00 – 1,200.00.

Stoneware

Stoneware in the United States is largely a product of the nineteenth century. Before 1800 redware was more popular and after 1900 new innovations and inventions essentially destroyed the handcrafted stoneware market.

Almost all American stoneware is flawed to some extent. Pitchers, jugs, crocks, churns, milk pans, and batter jugs were in use every day and often suffered from the experience. The actual process of making the stoneware pieces at the pottery was almost impossible to control and many examples were damaged to varying degrees in the firing process. The level of quality control in the American art pottery industry was vastly superior to that of the utilitarian stoneware industry. The utilitarian stoneware was designed to be functional and useful and not for display.

Cracks

a. drying lines — these are largely cosmetic and happened while the piece was being dried before being placed in the kiln. They are minor.
b. hairline — a crack that does not go "through," more of a fracture than a break. Problems can happen because the hairline has the potential to become a "through" crack over time.
c. through — light can pass through. Collectors usually pass on a marginal piece of stoneware with "through" cracks. They can be repaired at significant expense in relation to the value of the piece.
The more elaborate and unusual the cobalt decoration on a piece of stoneware, the more valuable the piece. A simple swirl or flower cannot be cracked or damaged significantly and hold its value. A scene with a deer, trees, and a house can sustain damage and cracks and still be very valuable. Decoration is the primary ingredient in value followed by condition, form, and maker (pottery). A decorated milk pan or a cooler with decoration is rarer than a crock or jug. Keep in mind that nineteenth century stoneware was utilitarian and not produced for decoration in the home. It was in daily use and thrown away and replaced very quickly when cracked, chipped, or dropped. It was inexpensive and usually plentiful.

Cosmetic Concerns

a. Burns or brown spots are caused by the piece being to close to the fire. The heat burns away the glaze to the surface of the stoneware.
b. "Fried" cobalt is caused by an overheated kiln and too much water in the cobalt slip. This causes the cobalt decoration to lose focus or blur, bubble, or burn away.

c. Too much heat in the kiln can also turn the cobalt blue to a black or even enhance the blurring or focus of the decoration. This can have a serious and negative effect on the value of the piece.
d. If there was too much salt in the kiln and the firing process cooled off too quickly, greenish bubbles can be found on the piece of stoneware. These can be described as "salt tears."
e. A craze is a crack in the glaze that doesn's affect the body of the stoneware. If you purchased a glazed donut and the frosting was cracked, the donut would still be perfectly intact.
f. At the height of the firing process rock salt was thrown into the kiln. It formed a vapor (fog) that settled over all the pieces of stoneware in the kiln. This served as a clear seal or waterproof barrier on the exterior of the piece. Brown slip (clay and water mixture like soup) was poured in and out of the piece to line the interior and serve as another waterproof barrier. This clay was often from the Hudson River near Albany, N.Y., and was called "Albany" slip.

A Brief Stoneware Glossary of Significant Terms

greenware — air dried pottery, unfired, ready for the kiln.

glaze — a thin, glasslike coating that seals the piece and provides a smooth, orange peel surface, created by rock salt vapor (fog) under intense heat.

ovoid — a pear shape of the earliest pieces of nineteenth century stoneware, broad shoulders to a narrow base. The more ovoid, the earlier the piece of stoneware, is generally accu rate. As the nineteenth century wore on, pieces of stoneware (especially jugs) became more cylindrical in form.

thrower — the individual (usually a male) who sits at the wheel and forms (throws) the pottery.

slip — finely grained clay turned to a thick soup by adding water and a coloring agent (ground cobalt oxide). Used to deco rate stoneware.

capacity mark — a number painted, incised, stamped (impressed), stenciled, or slip-trailed onto the wet clay that tells us the buyer of the piece the approximate size of the crock, jug, jar, or churn. The mark is typically expressed in gallons.

thrown — a piece of clay that has been placed on a potter's wheel and turned into a crock, jug, etc., by the craftsman's hands and skill. The opposite of molded.

molded — a technique used in potteries during the factory period to make thousands rather than hundreds of pieces a day. A mechanical process rather than a handmade production.

cooler-fountain — a large stoneware container for several or many gallons of cider, beer, or water with a spigot.

Decorating Techniques

a. incising — late 1700s until mid-1830s. A metal tool or sharp piece of wire is used to scratch a decoration into the body of a jug or crock. Could be complex with ships and flags, animals, scenes, people, or flowers. Rare and seriously expensive when found. The process of incising gradually disappeared because it was very labor intensive and as competition increased among potteries other methods of decoration were used. Many decorators (mostly women) were paid by the piece and incising took time.

b. slip-trailing or cupping — similar to decorating a cake by pouring a thin line of slip on the surface of the stoneware. It leaves a raised line of cobalt on the surface. The best of the slip-trailing was done in the 1850s and 1860s but it was popular from about 1840 to 1900.

c. brushed decoration — a very common technique in use between 1850 and the 1880s with the golden age the 1865 – 1875 period. It involves dipping a brush in cobalt slip and painting the surface of the stoneware. Elaborate pieces from the 1880s usually specially ordered to celebrate an anniversary or retirement were semi-expensive. As the century wore on the cost of labor and competition made the brushed decorating process less complex each year.

d. stenciling and transfer — this was the bitter end of the history of decorated stoneware in America. Often done on molded pieces from the 1880s into the twentieth century. Quick, neutral, inexpensive, and it required neither artistic talent nor judgment. The "paper or plastic" of stoneware production.

e. It is important to keep in mind that decorating techniques did not begin and end on any kind of a specific schedule. There were outposts and decorators who had styles that lingered over long periods. The special order pieces also tend to muddy the picture about when some spectacular pieces of stoneware were made and decorated.

The Death of American Stoneware Potteries

1. The development of home refrigeration (ice boxes).
2. Mass production of inexpensive glass containers.
3. Prohibition of the sale of beer and alcohol.
4. Potteries making specialty items rather than a whole line of stoneware products.

Basic Information for Collectors of American Utilitarian Pottery

— Stoneware color is dictated by the mix of clays in its production. Some potteries used expensive clay from New Jersey and mixed it with local clays. Others used stoneware clay available in their specific areas.

— Stoneware potteries were in operation in New York by 1775.
— Stoneware potteries fired their products at 2,100 degrees Fahrenheit. Redware, a much more fragile product, was fired at 1,700 degrees Fahrenheit. The brick kilns were wood fired and burned up to 30 – 36 hours when filled with product.
— The interiors of stoneware jugs, jars, crocks, and bottles were lined with brown clay called "Albany" slip. The slip was poured into and out of the piece to provide an interior of defense or sealing agent against liquids escaping. Vitrification refers to the ability of stoneware not to absorb liquids stored inside. Stoneware is vitreous and redware is not.
— Redware potteries came with the seventeenth century colonists of North America from Europe. The red clays were dug from swamps and creek beds so it was readily available. The problem was the soft lead glaze used to seal the plates, jugs, and bowls. Over time the glaze tended to fall away into the contents and create major health issues over a long period.
— Sgraffito (scratched ware) is a decorative form of redware. The designs were scratched or incised into the surface of the piece through the coating of slip. Sgraffito was not used in the households of the period in daily life but primarily was displayed as a decorative accessory. Decorated redware that was in daily use had decoration that was flush with the surface of the piece and not raised.
— Very rarely is redware signed by its maker. One notable exception is the Bell Pottery of Pennsylvania.
— There were redware potters making pie plates as late as 1900 with little change from examples of a century earlier. Simple pieces of utilitarian redware are difficult to accurately date.
— The bottoms of redware and stoneware pieces are always unglazed because if they were glazed they would become a permanent part of the kiln.
— Cobalt oxide was rarely (if ever) used with redware for decoration as it commonly was with stoneware because it turns black when fired.
— As a general rule the most highly decorated stoneware that is treasured by pottery and folk art collectors today tended to come from areas (New York State) where there was the most competition. The only thing that made utilitarian stoneware any better than yours was the quality of the decoration on it. Stoneware is stoneware, but decorated stoneware is unique and special. The more unusual and special the decoration the more significant the value of the piece.

Illustrations

It is also possible to date a piece of stoneware fairly closely by the name of the pottery. City directories give these names and the years they were in operation. The various potteries, for example, in Bennington, Vermont, produced wares under different names for most of the nineteenth century. Those pieces can be reasonably dated by the pottery name impressed into the piece.

We are going to use quarters of the nineteenth century for our purposes. It's close enough and, in some instances, less of a guess or estimate. For example:

first quarter — 1800 – 1820s
second quarter — 1830 – 1850s
third quarter — 1850s – 1870s
fourth quarter — late 1870s – early 1900s

If the maker's name is on the piece, we will include it and a current approximate value. It is *important* that we assume that each piece pictured is structurally sound with no major cracks, splits, or repairs that would negatively influence its value.

In the real world each piece of stoneware that you are considering adding to your collection must be closely inspected and evaluated. The pictures that follow will illustrate a world that may not be completely real but for our purposes it is the best way to convey a general understanding.

Two gallon jug, Geddes, New York, fourth quarter nineteenth century, $375.00 – 450.00.

Three gallon crock, J. Burger Jr., Rochester, New York, third quarter nineteenth century, $450.00 – 600.00.

One gallon pitcher, Lyons, New York, third quarter nineteenth century, brushed flower, $1,000.00 – 1,500.00.
One gallon pitcher, J. Burger Jr., Rochester, New York, cobalt wreath, slip-trailed decoration, third quarter nineteenth century, $1,000.00 – 1,500.00.

Four-gallon butter churn, cobalt bellflower, Cortland, New York, third quarter nineteenth century, impressed maker's mark, $1,300.00 – 1,600.00.

Five-gallon churn, J. Burger Jr., Rochester, New York, slip-trailed decoration, third quarter nineteenth century, $2,200.00 – 2,500.00.

Beehive-shaped jug, Whitmore, Havana, New York, third quarter nineteenth century, bird on plume decoration, two-gallon, $1,000.00 – 1,300.00.

Four-gallon crock, C.W. Braun, Buffalo, New York, deep cobalt double flower, slip-trailed decoration, early third quarter nineteenth century, $800.00 – 1,200.00.

Two-gallon jar, Ottman Brothers, Fort Edward, New York, bird on a branch, third quarter nineteenth century, $700.00 – 850.00.

Bale-handled pancake batter jug, flower decoration, probably New York state, third quarter nineteenth century, $600.00 – 800.00. Note: The majority of batter jugs are found without decoration and are generally not marked by the maker. The tin lid and pouring spout cover are seldom part of the package.

Six-gallon Braun crock, slip-trailed bird, rare detailed decoration, Buffalo, New York, early third quarter nineteenth century, $3,500.00 – 5,000.00.

Two-gallon cream pot, J. and E. Norton, Bennington, Vermont, bird on a branch, 1850 – 1861, $1,200.00 – 1,600.00.

Four-gallon crock, slip-trailed chicken pecking corn, no maker's mark, impressed capacity mark, third quarter nineteenth century, excellent condition, $1,500.00 – 2,200.00.

One-gallon jug, C. Crolius, Manhattan Wells, New York (New York City), first quarter nineteenth century, classic ovoid form, $2,200.00 – 2,800.00. Note: As the nineteenth century grinds forward, the stoneware jugs become more cylindrical in form. Crolius is a very serious mark.

One-gallon jug, J. & E. Norton, Bennington, Vermont, tree decoration, 1850 – 1861, $2,400.00 – 2,800.00.

Three-gallon cream pot, T. Harrington, Lyons, New York, double capacity marks and flowers, touch of cobalt on applied ears or handles, third quarter nineteenth century, $700.00 – 900.00.

Classic slip-trailed "love birds," S. Hart, Fulton, New York, early third quarter nineteenth century, $1,400.00 – 1,750.00.

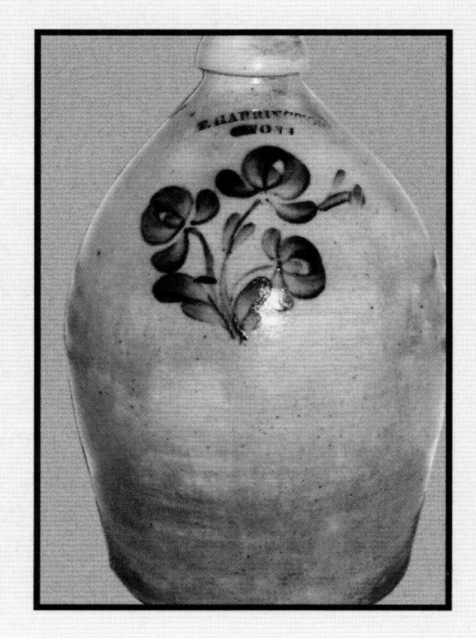

Three-gallon jug, brushed flowers, T. Harrington, Lyons, New York, third quarter nineteenth century, $650.00 – 725.00.

Two-gallon jug, E. & L.P. Norton, Bennington, Vermont, bird decoration, 1861 – 1881, $1,700.00 – 1,900.00.
Note: The burn at the base has been with the piece since it was fired in the kiln.

Lid from a butter crock with brushed decoration, c. third quarter of the nineteenth century, 14" in diameter, $325.00 – 400.00.
Note: Lids are much more difficult to find than the crocks they were paired with about 1870. The lids and crocks were made independently (probably on different days) and then matched. The potter could have made sized crocks on Friday and sized lids on Tuesday. The lids and crocks are seldom found with a potter's mark and are often decorated with a few swipes of a brush dipped in cobalt slip. Possibly Pennsylvania in origin.

Five-gallon crock, Gedes, New York (Syracuse), with "dotted" slip-trailed deer, early fourth quarter of the nineteenth century, rare, $6,000.00 – 8,500.00.

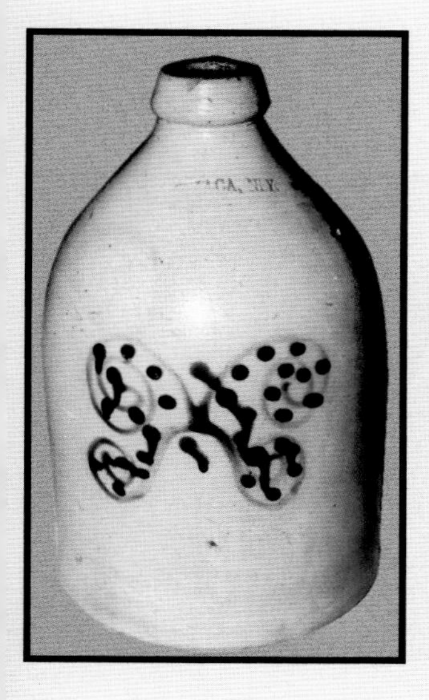

Jug, Utica, New York, slip-trailed "butterfly," two-gallon, third quarter nineteenth century, $330.00 – 450.00.

Three-gallon cream pot, T. Harrington, Lyons, New York, slip-trailed eight-pointed star and face, third quarter nineteenth century, $7,000.00 – 9,000.00.

Signed pitcher, Binghamton, New York, lined with Albany slip, slip-trailed floral decoration, early fourth quarter nineteenth century, $1,400.00 – 1,600.00.
Note: This example has the "pinched" pouring spout.

Cuspidor or spittoon, brushed decoration on unmarked stoneware for "home" use, probably New York state, early fourth quarter nineteenth century, $600.00 – 700.00.

Two-gallon crock, bird decorated, Haxstun and Co., Fort Edward, New York, early fourth quarter nineteenth century, $700.00 – 1,000.00.

Cream pot, West Troy, New York, three-gallon impressed capacity, flower and "butterfly" stem, applied ear handles, fourth quarter nineteenth century, $900.00 – 1,100.00.

Two-gallon cream pot, cobalt floral decoration, Clinton Pottery, third quarter nineteenth century, $625.00 – 750.00.
Note: This is an example of a piece with a "focus" issue on the cobalt flowers. To some degree it has a negative effect on the value.

Four-gallon crock, elaborate scene with cobalt deer, Lyons, New York, third quarter nineteenth century, $5,000.00 – 7,000.00.

Pitcher, John Burger, Rochester, New York, cabbage flower, early third quarter nineteenth century, $2,500.00 – 3,500.00.

Three-gallon crock, J. Norton, Bennington, Vermont, chicken pecking corn, third quarter nineteenth century, $2,500.00 – 3,000.00. Note: For some mysterious reason the chickens tend to peck to their right (viewer's left).

Crock, John Burger, Rochester, New York, double cobalt flower, deep slip-trailed decoration, early third quarter of the nineteenth century, $1,800.00 – 2,200.00.

Five-gallon cream pot, Farrar, Geddes, New York, huge cobalt floral decoration, third quarter nineteenth century, $1,500.00 – 1,800.00.

Two-gallon crock, New York, state bluebird on a branch, unsigned, fourth quarter nineteenth century, $800.00 – 1,200.00.

One-gallon cream pot, J. and E. Norton, Bennington, Vermont, bold cobalt decoration, 1850 – 1861, $1,400.00 – 1,600.00.

Two, three-gallon crocks, Burgerand Lang, Rochester, New York, cobalt wreaths, both done by the same decorator, late third quarter nineteenth century, $800.00 – 950.00 (each).

Unusual one-gallon crock, Clark and Co. Rochester, New York, third quarter nineteenth century, $700.00 – 850.00. **One-gallon jar,** Clark and Co., third quarter nineteenth century, $700.00 – 850.00.

Bold four-gallon crock, Mantell and Thomas, Penn Yan, New York, deep cobalt decoration, slip-trailed, late second quarter nineteenth century, $1,200.00 – 1,500.00.

Four gallon jug, J. Fisher, Lyons, New York, slip-trailed dragonfly, fourth quarter nineteenth century, $400.00 – 485.00.

Three-gallon jug, Fort Edward, New York, impressed capacity mark and bold cobalt decoration, $800.00 – 950.00.

Preserve jar, John Burger, two-gallon, slip-trailed capacity mark, floral decoration, early third quarter nineteenth century, $1,100.00 – 1,350.00.

Four-gallon crock, Burger Bros., Rochester, New York, third quarter nineteenth century, $800.00 – 1,000.00.

Rare two-gallon jug, West Troy, New York, with feeding bird, late third quarter nineteenth century, $1,800.00 – 2,200.00.

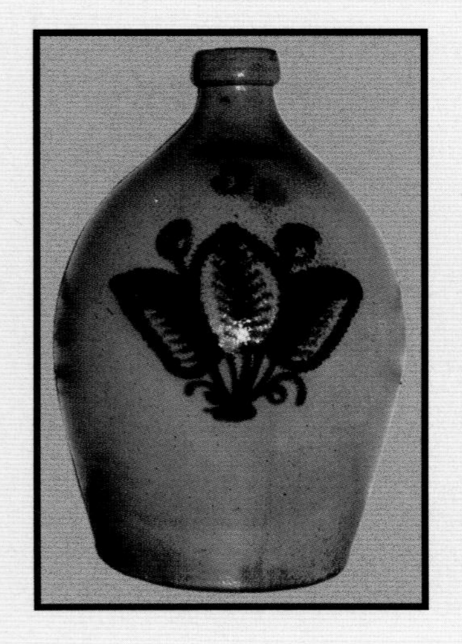

Three-gallon jug, John Burger, Rochester, New York, cobalt fern leaf, early third quarter nineteenth century, $725.00 – 900.00.

Six-quart crock, J. Norton, Bennington, Vermont, bluebird, 1859 – 1861, rare, $1,600.00 – 2,000.00.

Two-gallon crock, J. Fisher, Lyons, New York, brushed flower, fourth quarter nineteenth century, $585.00 – 675.00.

Two-gallon preserve jar, John Burger, Rochester, New York, bold cobalt flower, third quarter nineteenth century, $1,200.00 – 1,400.00.

Six-gallon butter churn, Havana, New York, third quarter nineteenth century, $3,500.00 – 5,000.00.
Six-gallon crock, H.M. Whitman, Havana, New York, with grapes and cobalt vines, third quarter nineteenth century, $3,500.00 – 4,500.00.

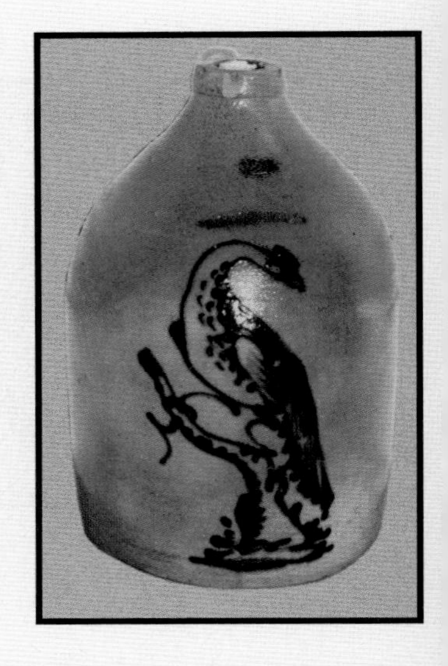

Two-gallon jug, bird on a stump, Whites, Utica, New York, early fourth quarter nineteenth century, $3,000.00 – 4,000.00.

Five-gallon Butter Churn, J. Burger Jr., Rochester, New York, slip-trailed decoration, unique capacity mark in flower, third quarter nineteenth century, $2,200.00 – 2,800.00.
Six-gallon churn, N. Clark and Company, oversized cobalt floral decoration, late third quarter nineteenth century, $2,000.00 – 2,600.00.

Three-gallon crock, Buffalo, New York, great winged Braun, early third quarter nineteenth century, slip-trailed decoration, $4,000.00 – 6,000.00.

Two-gallon jug, S. Hart, Fulton, New York, "beehive" form, unusual cobalt design, third quarter nineteenth century, $800.00 – 1,000.00.
Two-gallon crock, Burger Bros., Rochester, New York, third quarter nineteenth century, $650.00 – 850.00.

One-gallon crock, F.B. Norton, Worcester, Massachusetts, dark bluebird, rare size, after 1865, $1,000.00 – 1,300.00.

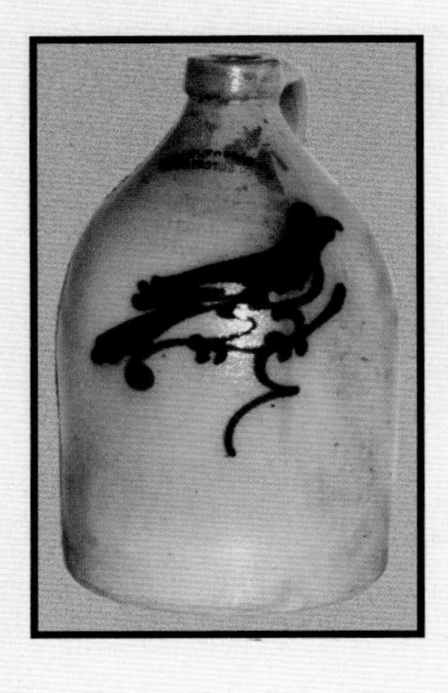

One-gallon jug, J. & E. Norton, Bennington, Vermont, cobalt bird, 1850 – 1859, $1,000.00 – 1,300.00.

One-gallon jug, N.A. White and Son, Utica, New York, slip-trailed Christmas or pine tree, late third quarter nineteenth century, $500.00 – 600.00.

Two-gallon jug, White and Son, Utica, New York, Christmas tree, slip-trailed cobalt decoration, neatly impressed maker's mark, late third quarter nineteenth century, $500.00 – 600.00.

Three-gallon jug, J. Burger Jr., Rochester, New York, with cobalt brushed grapes, early third quarter nineteenth century, $1,000.00 – 1,500.00.

Six-gallon crock, cobalt basket of flowers, J. & E. Norton, Bennington, Vermont, 1850 – 1859, $3,500.00 – 4,500.00.

Rare "man in the moon" jug, brushed cobalt, Pennsylvania, third quarter nineteenth century, $5,000.00 – 7,000.00.

Slip-trailed "Fish" crock, Havana, New York, Whitman, early third quarter nineteenth century, two gallons, $5,000.00 – 6,000.00.

Three-gallon preserve jar, with detailed cobalt bird on a floral branch, impressed mark, third quarter nineteenth century, $2,800.00 – 3,200.00.

Special order pitcher, possibly a marriage, anniversary, or retirement gift, early third quarter nineteenth century, $4,000.00 – 5,000.00.

Unusual ovoid one-gallon jar, Lyons, New York, with lid, early third quarter nineteenth century, $700.00 – 900.00.

Two-gallon jug, J. Norton, Bennington, Vermont, bluebird, 1859 – 1861, $900.00 – 1,100.00.

Two-gallon crock, E. & L.P. Norton, Bennington, Vermont, floral spray, 1861 – 1881, $500.00 – 675.00.

Two-gallon pitcher, J. & E. Norton, "pinched" spout, cobalt floral spray, 1850 – 1859, $1,300.00 – 1,600.00.

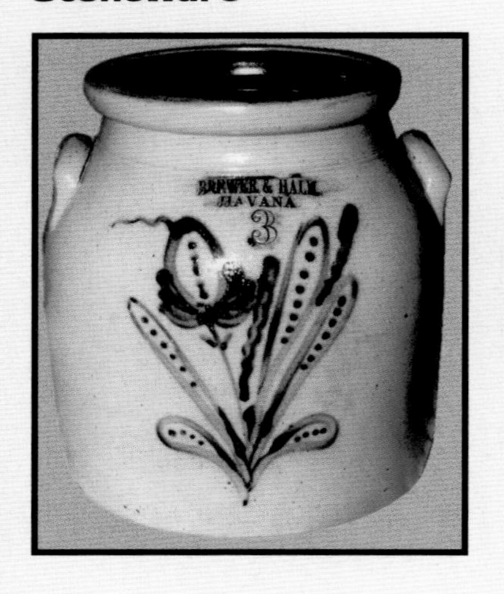

Three-gallon jar, Brewer & Halm, Havana, New York, cobalt flower, late third quarter nineteenth century, $800.00 – 1,200.00.

Unmarked pitcher, heavily decorated, probably Pennsylvania in origin, third quarter nineteenth century, $2,200.00 – 2,500.00.

Cake crock, unmarked, probably Pennsylvania, early third quarter nineteenth century, brushed cobalt decoration, 13" diameter, $900.00 – 1,300.00.

Lidded jar, Clark and Co. slip-trailed flower, third quarter nineteenth century, $500.00 – 625.00.

The Absolute Basics of Collecting Stoneware Bottles

— Rarely, if ever, is the potter's name on the bottle. If there is a name, it is the seller's or the product impressed on the bottle.
— The bottles went from the potter to the wholesaler and were seldom sold directly to the consumers.
— The primary product in the stoneware bottle was a variety of beer, ale, or soda pop.
— After the mid-1850s, most stoneware bottles were molded rather than hand thrown.
— Bottles are found in sizes ranging from 8 ounces to 32 ounces with additional odd sizes thrown into the mix. There is a 46 ounce pop bottle known that has to be among the largest ever discovered.
— The date that is impressed into the bottle is when the product was originally established, not when the bottle was molded.
— After the mid-1850s stoneware bottles were molded with a tapered cylindrical body in one mold and joined with a conical neck and lip formed in a second mold.

Stoneware

— The stoneware bottle market was gradually extinguished by glass liquor, beer, and patent medicine bottles that were plentiful and cheap.
— The advantage of stoneware bottles was that they could be easily reused and also they kept the contents chilled when taken out of cold storage.
— Plain, unmarked stoneware bottles are usually offered for $15.00 – 40.00.
— A bottle with the bottler's name or product is $35.00 – 65.00.
— The bottler's name, product, date, and location make it worth $125.00 – 150.00.
— The addition of hand inscribed cobalt lettering usually makes it a $175.00 – 325.00 item.
— Bottles made of stoneware dated after 1890 would certainly be uncommon because of the mass production of glass vessels that closed most stoneware bottle makers.
— The stamp that was impressed into the wet clay was sometimes dipped in blue cobalt slip to add a hint of color.
— The cobalt that is found on bottles was usually quickly brushed on.
— The bar owner or storekeeper usually filled the bottles himself from a vat or barrel in the basement.
— Molded bottles with 12 sides were a much more involved process than conventional molding and are not commonly found.
— Stoneware flasks are much rarer, earlier, and more expensive than stoneware bottles.

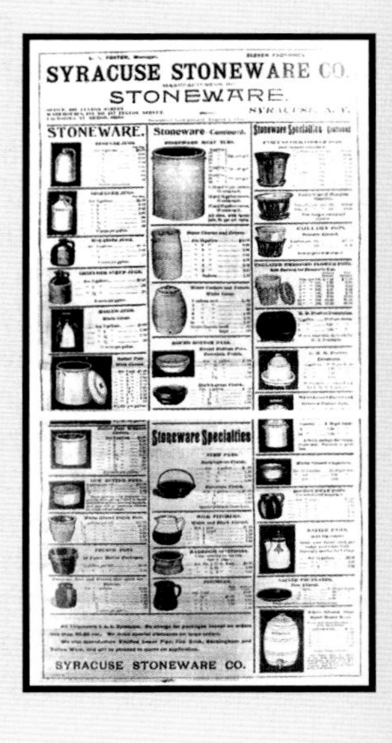

Top: **Unmarked,** $25.00; **Wright City Beer,** $55.00; **unmarked with a splash of cobalt,** $40.00; **plain bottle with impressed mark,** $50.00; **cobalt lip and bottler's name and "Bottle Not Sold" impressed**, $135.00.
Bottom: **Cobalt splash,** $40.00; **"W.W.,"** $135.00; **"M & S" impressed with light cobalt,** $85.00; **conical neck and lip dipped in cobalt and impressed lettering**, $135.00; **light cobalt lip and impressed "Sugar Ale,"** $110.00.

"Hand Thrown" vs. Molded Stoneware

A comparison of advertising broadsides from the Honesdale Pennsylvania Pottery in 1863 and the Syracuse Stoneware Company New York in 1900 illustrates where the American stoneware industry went.

Honesdale 1863	6 gallon churn $15 a dozen ($1.75 each)
Syracuse 1900	6 gallon churn $5.88 a dozen
Honesdale 1863	5 gallon jug $12 a dozen ($1.35 each)
Syracuse 1900	5 gallon jug $4.80 a dozen
Honesdale 1863	12" spittoon $6 a dozen
Syracuse 1900	12" spittoon $4 a dozen

A pottery that depended on skilled craftsmen to throw stoneware on a wheel could not possibly compete with mass-produced and molded stoneware products. The quality of the pieces from the two potteries was not different but the costs involved in the manufacturing process were huge. Note that the 1863 dollar also bought considerably more than the 1900 dollar.

Shortly after 1900 the molded stoneware industry is going to take serious hits from expanding glass factories, home refrigerator, and a national prohibition of alcohol sales that killed the stoneware bottle business.

Watt Pottery

Watt sign, 1994, $100.00.

(This section was prepared by Mary Lynn Edwards. Ms Edwards can be reached at papermoon2@verizon.net)

It was 1983 and my first flea market. At one of the first booths I entered, I spotted a pitcher with a design that I recognized. It caught my eye because I had two pitchers at home with the exact pattern — a gift from my mother-in-law ten years before as we were helping her move. In fact, I was using one of them every day to serve orange juice at breakfast.

I picked up the pitcher and looked at it, thinking it would be nice to give to my recently married daughter as a housewarming gift. Then I looked at the price and to my amazement it was priced at $85.00. I immediately sought out the dealer and he told me that the pitcher was the apple design made by Watt Pottery from Crooksville, Ohio, from 1936 to 1965 when the plant burned down.

I continued on my way, sans pitcher, but in other booths I found several other Watt items and decided then and there that I wanted to use this pattern to decorate my kitchen. By the time I returned home, I had increased my Watt collection by three more pieces — a pie plate, a smaller pitcher, and a bowl. I also retired the juice pitcher from everyday use. I bought a good reference book and now my collection includes many pieces that sit atop my kitchen cabinets.

In 1995, I bought several pieces at an auction and discovered that they were recent reproductions. It was hard to tell at first glance, but with the help of information provided to me by a fellow collector, I learned to tell the old from the new. Much to my relief, after using this info to examine my entire collection, none of my other pieces were reproductions. However, my enthusiasm for the pottery waned and I am much more cautious in my purchases.

The bad news about the reproductions is that one cannot really determine the age from the mark on the bottom. The good news is that there are other indications that one can use to verify age. For example, on new pitchers there is a pronounced dimple on the inside of the item where the handle meets the body. The old ones generally do not have this dimple. The pattern itself yields clues. On the old, the branches vary in width while on the new the branches don't show this variation. There are other differences and the website www.repronews.com has this information (subscription only).

The Watt Pottery Collector's Association was organized in 1992 and has more than 1,500 members. The annual membership dues of $20 brings a quarterly newsletter and admission to the Watt Pottery Auction at the convention.

Two-handled bean pot, Watt # 76, 7½", 5½" lid, $135.00.

Ribbed covered bowl, Watt # 601, 8¾", 3½" lid, $125.00.

Stick-handled individual casserole, 5¼" 3¾" lid, $150.00.

Left to right: **Cereal Bowl,** Watt # 52, 6½", 2", $35.00;
Mixing Bowl, Watt # 5, 5", 2⅞", $55.00;
Mixing Bowl, Watt # 63, 6⅜", 4¼", $55.00.

Barrel-shaped salt and pepper, 2½", 4¼", pair, $160.00.

Left to right: **Mixing bowl,** 7", 3", $55.00;
Mixing bowl, 6", 3½", $55.00.

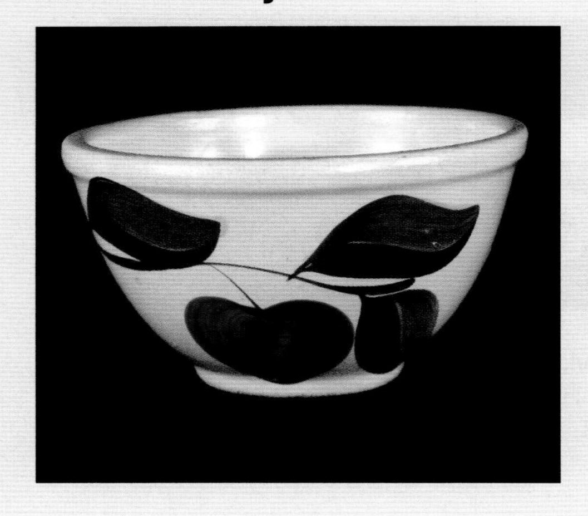

Mixing bowl, Watt # 6, 6", 3½", $55.00.

Mixing bowl, writing inside, Watt # 6, 6", 3½", $55.00.

Left to right: **Mixing Bowl,** Watt # 7, 7", 4" $55.00; **Mixing Bowl,** Watt # 8, 8", 4½", $55.00; **Mixing Bowl,** Watt # 9, 9¼", 5", $55.00.

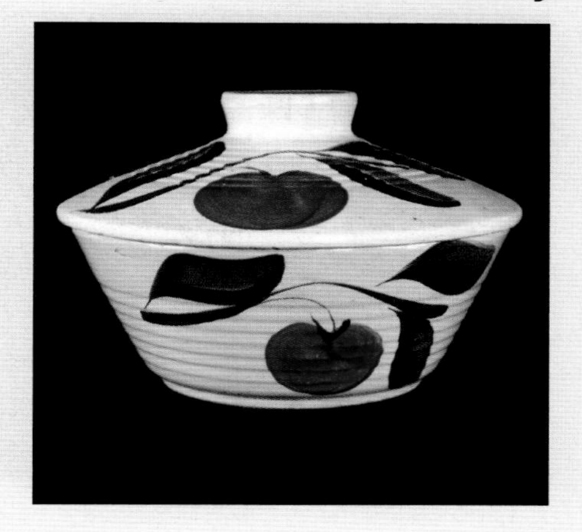

Ribbed covered bowl, Watt # 601, 8½", 6½", lid, $125.00.

Creamer, Watt # 62, 5", 2", $110.00;
Pitcher, Watt # 15, 5¼", $55.00;
Pitcher, Watt # 16, 6½", $110.00.

French-handled casserole, Watt # 18, 4", 5", lid, $225.00.

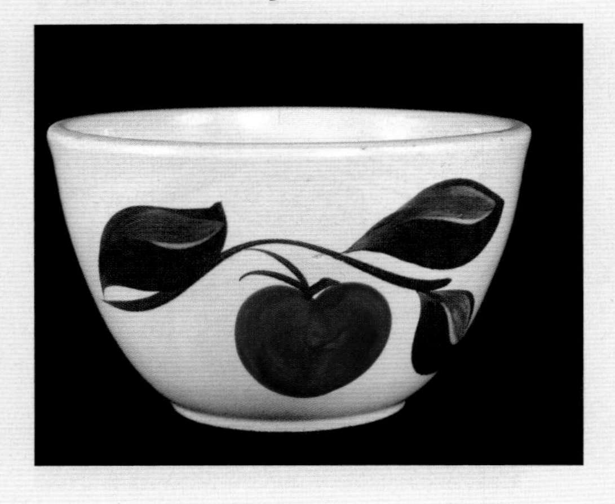

Mixing bowl, Watt # 64, 7½", 4⅞", $55.00.

Mixing bowl, Watt # 65, 9", 5½", lid, $75.00.

Cereal/salad bowl, Watt # 74, 5½", 2", $35.00.

Bowl, Watt # 5, 7½", 4¾", $55.00

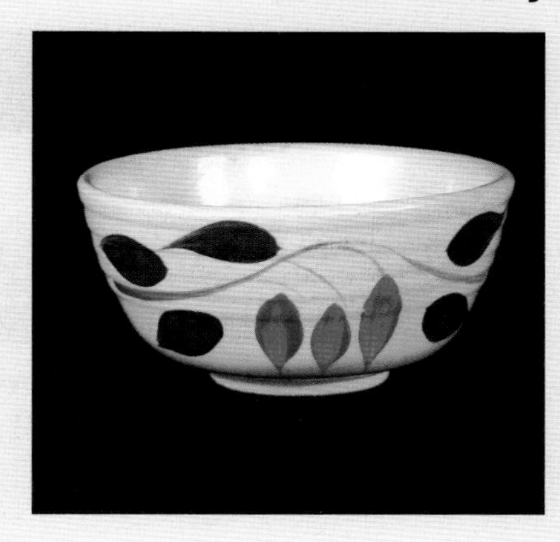

Bottom view of above.

Individual bean server, Watt # 75, 3¾", 2¼", $75.00.

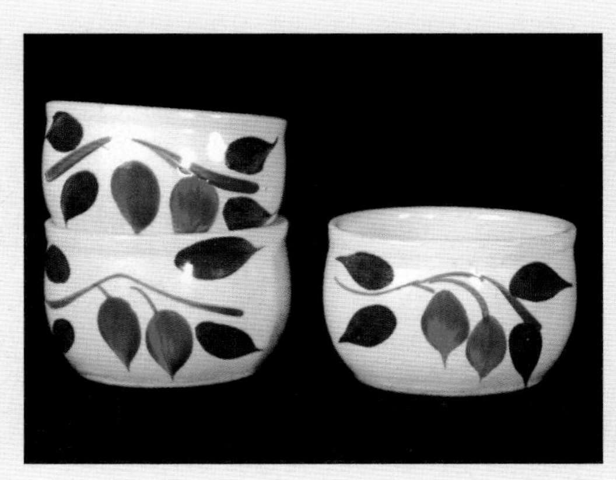

Left to right: Ribbed Mixing Bowl, Watt # 4, 4", 2¼", $55.00; **Ribbed Mixing Bowl,** Watt # 602, 4¾", 1½", $65.00.

Pie plate, Watt # 33, 9", 1⅞" $175.00.

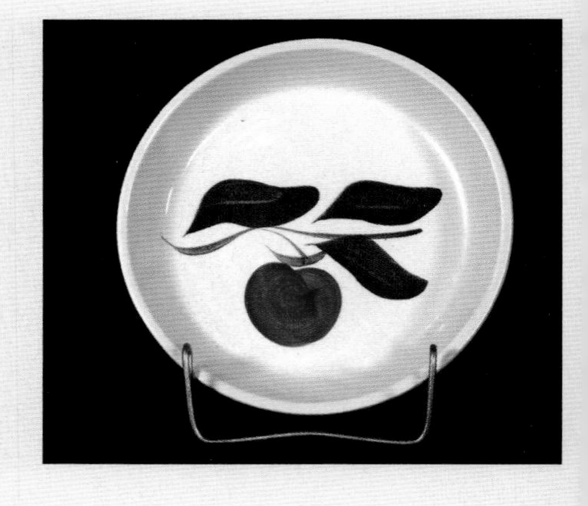

Bottom view of pie plate.

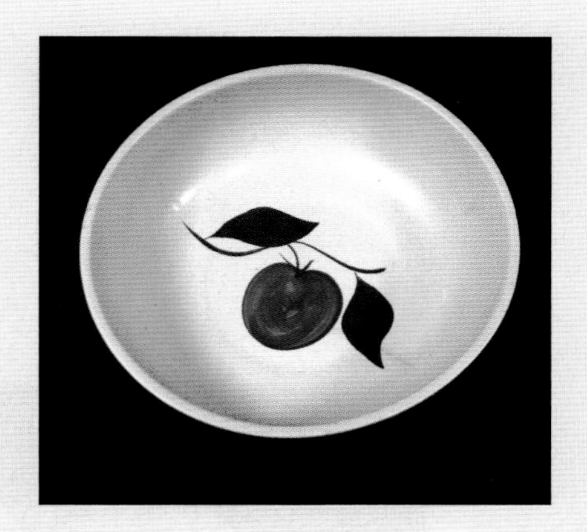

Bowl, Watt # 55, 12", 4", a crack or chip would reduce the value a minimum of 50% to 60%. $200.00.

Spaghetti bowl, Watt # 39, 13", 4", lid, $175.00.

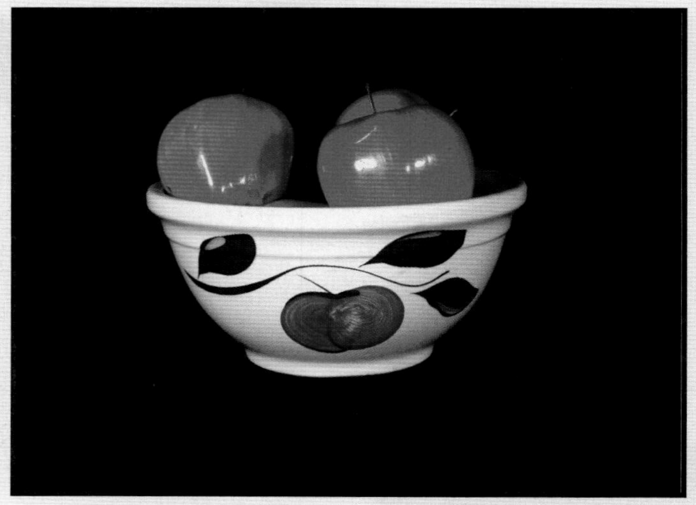

Mixing bowl, Watt # 8, 8", 4", $55.00.

Windmill Weights

Windmill weights.

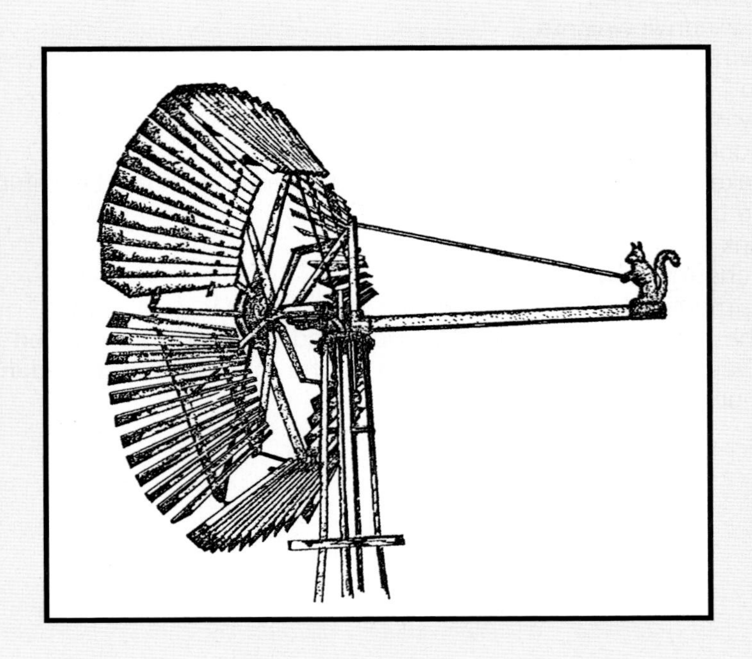

Windmill Weights

About 1970, on the way back to Illinois from visiting friends in colorful Colorado, we stopped for gasoline somewhere in Nebraska. As we pulled out of the dusty parking lot after filling the tank with 36¢ gasoline, we noticed a crude sign nailed to a telephone post that read "Antiques ½ mile" with an arrow. We were not in a hurry so we drove down the dusty gravel road to a weathered farmhouse. An elderly lady was pushing a rotary blade mower around 60 – 100 cast-iron figures in the front yard. The grass hadn't been cut in a while so she was working. She stopped and wiped her face with a napkin from a pocket in her dress.

"What?"

"Pardon me, are you open?"

"Depends."

"On what. . . ?"

"What do you want?"

"What are those cast iron figures?"

"Windmill weights."

"Window weights?"

"No, windmill weights."

"How much are they?"

"$25."

"How much if I bought two?"

"50 dollars."

"I'll take the horse with the jockey and the cow with the broken tail."

"It's a bull."

"Thank you."

"No checks, only cash."

"Yes, madam."

The jointed jockey and the bridle had been probably added after the Dempster bob-tail came down off the mill and was turned in to a yard ornament.

Notes for Weight Collectors

1. The Holy Grail would be a salesman's sample windmill with a cast-iron weight.
2. Figural weights are counterbalance or tail weights. They counter balance the weight of the wheel.
3. The weights with roosters, bulls, squirrels, or horses served as advertisements for the company that made the windmills in addition to counterbalances.
4. Few are ever found with "original" paint because exposure to weather over a decade strips any surface of paint. The "repaints" were created after the weight became a driveway or yard ornament.
5. Paint is sometimes added to reproductions to mask the obvious.
6. The windmill was especially popular on farms west of the Mississippi River in the period between 1880 and the 1930s.
7. World War I and World War II scrap drives and electricity coming to the farm in the 1930s caused many weights and mills to disappear.
8. It is not uncommon to find a reproduction weight with a surface of sand mixed with legitimate rust scraped from another cast iron implement that earned its rust legitimately.
9. The reproductions are usually lighter in weight and smaller in size than originals because they are cast from molds made from the original weight.
10. The fact that windmill weights were cast in molds and not created by an individual artist's hands make the designation as "American folk art" open to serious discussion.
11. Different geographical sections of North America produce different colors, textures, and shades of rust because of temperatures, acid rain, moisture, and wind conditions.
12. The first article about windmill weights (probably) was published in *Spinning Wheel Magazine* in March of 1967.

Quick Guide to Makers

roosters — Elgin (IL) Wind Power and Pump
horses — Dempster Mill of Beatrice, Nebraska
bulls — Fairbury, Nebraska, Dempster Manufacturing of Des Moines, Iowa
squirrel — Elgin Wind Power and Pump
star — U.S. Wind Engine and Pump of Batavia, Illinois
star — Flint and Walling, Kendallville, Indiana (on a cast iron disk)
warship and football of concrete and cast iron— Baker Manufacturing of Evansville, Wisconsin
letter "W" — Althouse-Wheeler, Waupun, Wisconsin

Dempster Manufacturing Co. bull, Des Moines, Iowa, broken tail, $500.00 – 575.00.

Bull, Fairbury Nebraska Windmill Co., 1910 – 1920, originally painted bold red, for 12' wheel, $2,200.00 – 2,600.00.

Bull, Fairbury for 10' wheel, 1910 – 1920, $2,000.00 – 2,500.00.

Bob-tail or short-tail horse, Dempster Mill Manufacturing Co., Beatrice Nebraska, 1900 – 1940. The long-tail horse was manufactured before the bob-tail. The horse's mane appears only on the right side on both horses. $800.00 – 1,000.00.

Star, U.S. Wind Engine and Pumping Co. of Batavia, Illinois, 1880s – 1916, used on wheel with 10' diameter, weighs 40 pounds, actually a counter balance weight, $3,000.00 – 3,500.00.

Star on a cylindrical governor weight, used on 12' Star Mill, 1880s – 1916, originally painted green, Flint and Walling, Kendallville, Indiana, $2,200.00 – 2,800.00.

"Rainbow tail" rooster, Elgin Wind Power and Pump Company, Elgin, Illinois, 60 pounds, $4,000.00 – 4,500.00.

Rooster, Elgin Wind Power and Pump Company, 1880s – 1890s, 53 pounds, "barnacle-eye," $4,000.00 – 5,000.00.

Hummer E 184 with ball-shaped base, rooster is 13¼" tall with a 6" stem, Elgin Wind Power, Elgin, Illinois, $1,000.00 – 1,200.00.

Short-stem rooster, Hummer rooster, Elgin Wind & Power, $1,000.00 – 1,200.00.

Final Evaluation

Entrance Examination
Americana Collectors Hall of Awareness

Read each question carefully and select the best answer. Your score will be recorded on the national data bank and subject to periodic review by an independent committee of your peers. They will be in contact with you indirectly on a need to know basis. At the moment you don't. If you do not want your file open to public inspection and discussion, promise to give up tomato soup.

1. The most commonly found pieces of furniture made by the Shakers are
a. hickory and maple lamp tables.
b. simple rod-back dining chairs.
c. pie safes from New England communities.
d. none of the above are correct.

2. American redware with cobalt slip decoration is
a. often discovered along towns served by the Erie Canal.
b. almost nonexistent.
c. less likely to chip than cobalt decorated stoneware products.
d. called sgraffito in Pennsylvania and West Virginia.

3. True or False — Depression glass was first made in the United States during the Great Panic of 1847 when banks and other financial institutions closed.

4. True or False — Antique Week in New Hampshire is held in August and the Heart of Country show is scheduled in Nashville in February.

5. The Old Hickory Furniture Company and a dozen other firms that made hickory lodge-type furnishings were located in
a. Indiana.
b. Illinois.
c. New York.
d. Binghamton.

6. True or False — An American flag with 48 stars was almost certainly made before 1961.

7. Canton blue and white porcelain was made
a. at the Canton Industrial Porcelain Company in Canton, Ohio.
b. and imported from the Cantoni Company in Sicily about 1730 – 1780.
c. in China.
d. largely in Manchester, England, from 1760 to 1850.

8. The term "highboy"
a. is English in origin and is a chest on tall legs with two to four drawers.
b. refers to a "high country" piece of furniture made of oak and maple.
c. is American in origin.
d. was made largely in Manchester, England, from 1810 to about 1870 and exported to several furniture distributors in Boston.

9. True or False — A cabriole-type leg is usually made from crotch walnut and straight.

10. If you compare an antique piece of American pewter with a piece of English pewter you will find
a. it's impossible to tell the difference.
b. American pewter is marked by its maker less often than English pewter.
c. that English copies of American pewter can cause serious problems for collectors.

11 True or False — If a couple got married in the 1930s or 1940s, it's possible they received a piece of Roseville Pottery made in San Francisco, California, on Palmetto Street as a wedding fit.

12. Eighteenth century Chippendale chairs were made of
a. mahogany.
b. pine, cherry, and poplar as a secondary wood.
c. fruitwood.
d. rosewood.

13. A baseball signed "Babe Ruth" in excellent to mint condition and dated 7-18-49 could be worth
a. $9,000.00.
b. at least $5,000.00.
c. worthless.
d. at least $5,000.00, and possibly much more if it is an official ball signed on the "sweet spot" in fountain pen along with a letter of authenticity.

14. True or False — Windsor chairs were first produced in the southern colonies and eventually sold in England in the late eighteenth century.

15. Blue Willow pattern transfer-ware always has
a. a willow tree, a figure, and four birds.
b. two birds, three figures, and a willow tree.
c. mountains, sky, two pagodas, and a sunset.
d. four figures on a bridge and a bird.

16. True or False — Bakelite is a combination of silver nitrate, brass, baking soda, and carbon oxides, and was used in the manufacture of plastic for jewelry and household appliances in the 1930s.

17. Press-molded glass that allowed inexpensive mass production of glass happened after
a. 1825.
b. 1850.
c. 1875.
d. 1900.

18. A cellaret was designed to hold
a. wine.
b. tools.
c. salt.
d. spices and/or sugar.

19. A hunt board is more likely to be found in
a. New Hampshire.
b. New Jersey.
c. Iowa.
d. Virginia.
e. widely distributed and could be in all of the above.

20. The marketing skills of Martha Stewart could favorably be compared to the work of
a. Russel Wright.
b. Ralph Dunbar.
c. Ronald S. Schieber.
d. Richard Wayne Esq.

Final Evaluation

Match the name with a letter to the proper description with a number.

21. potter
22. steamer trunks
23. teddy bears
24. lived from 1905 to 1990 and designed studio craft furniture
25. designed mass-produced, mid-century glassware
26. legendary mid-century chair designer
27. favorite color was green
28. American toy maker

a. Louis Viutton
b. Raymond Eames
c. George Nakashima
d. John Deere
e. Steiff
f. J. Norton
g. Russel Wright
h. Marx
i. S. Salowitz

NOTE: QUESTIONS 29 & 30 GO WITH PHOTO 2

29. This stoneware was decorated with a
a. brush.
b. sponge.
c. rag with pierced holes dipped in slip.
d. transfer.

30. True or False — The pitcher in the center would be valued at more than $200.00.

*** The following is a three-point bonus question that can be used to enhance your final grade on this test.**

In twenty words or less, please describe the relationship of Fawn Lebowitz to the rise of commercial stoneware in the United States of America. There should be at least one reference in your answer to Eric Stratton.

Answers

1. d
2. b
3. f
4. t
5. a
6. t
7. c
8. c
9. f
10. b
11. f
12. a
13. c Ruth died in 1948.
14. f
15. b
16. f
17. a
18. a
19. d
20. a
21. f
22. a
23. e
24. c
25. g
26. b
27. d
28. h
29. b
30. t

Bonus essay question — Fawn Lebowitz was a truly great American potter who died prematurely, instantly, and tragically on her college campus in a kiln explosion that destroyed her wares and a Dr. Pepper machine (vintage). Eric Stratton restored the machine painstakingly and established a scholarship for potential bottlers at the institution in Fawn's name.

Evaluating your Final Score

correct 0 – 10
Your name has been electronically forwarded to every underwear resale and thrift store in America. You are on the list.

correct 11 – 19
So sad, and with your education.

correct 20 – 25
With the payment of appropriate admission fees you will be admitted to any antiques show in America during its posted business hours.

correct 26 – 30
You will automatically receive a free autographed copy of all previous editions of this book as supplies allow.

* If you have questions, please ask the waitress.

Glossary

If you are going to repair the transmission on a 1949 Packard it's important that you have the correct tools and a general idea of the process. There are also some key words or phrases that you need to expedite the job and communicate with the man behind the parts counter at the Packard dealership or the grizzled owner of the junkyard holding the lurching pit bull.

If you are going to drop three or four figures on an early chair at an antiques event, it is quasi-important that you have a general idea of what you are purchasing and a passing familiarity with the words and phrases commonly used in the antiques and collectibles community.

The sampling of words that follow will assist you in negotiating a slippery and winding slope toward achieving minimal respect in your neighborhood collectibles study group. There is no question that you will know more than the old lady down the block with the fixation on her collection of contemporary Branson, Missouri, memorabilia and the purple hair.

Albany slip — a mixture of water and brown clay (slip) taken from the Hudson River that was used to line the interior of New York state stoneware. The "chocolate" colored mixture was also used on the exterior of some late nineteenth century stoneware.

antiques and collectibles mall — a group of dealers with a wide range of merchandise who rent spaces in a large building and offer their wares. An independent manager oversees the operation.

Antique Week in New Hampshire — a week of upscale antiques shows opening and closing over a seven-day period in Manchester and the vicinity. Held in August.

architectural — usually an adjective that describes a piece that was originally actually built into the home or building. Could be a cupboard or bookcase.

as found — exactly what the term suggests — a piece taken from a garage, basement, or barn in the same condition in which it is offered for sale with no changes.

attic finish — to some collectors this would suggest a higher quality than "as found" but similar in form. The same condition as the day it went into the attic.

Glossary

attribution — often a painting or piece of folk art will enter the market and an artist or maker is not known for certain. At that point previous known examples will be used for comparison and an "attribution" will be made. It could just as easily be a chair, cupboard, or piece of iron as a painting. Attributed to. . .

breadboard ends — strips of wood nailed or pinned to the ends of a tabletop to keep the boards that make up the top from cupping or warping.

Brimfield — a town in mid-Massachusetts that several times a year (spring, summer, and fall) takes a week out and turns into a destination point for several thousand dealers and 100,000 plus collectors from across America to attend a series of markets and shows opening and closing on a tightly prearranged schedule in relative close proximity.

brown furniture — typically used to describe an antiques show filled with period related furniture with similar finishes. At a "brown furniture" show Pez collectors may have a problem finding anything to purchase.

buyer's premium — an additional fee added to the cost of an item bought at auction. Paid by the buyer. If the auction selling price is $100 and there is a 15% buyer's premium, the check would be written to the auction house for $115 plus applicable taxes.

case piece — usually a bookcase, cupboard, large piece of wooden furniture that is going to take at least two individuals to move.

circa — about, refers to an approximate time that usually gives some room for discussion. For example, c. 1840 means that the item probably dates from 1820 to the late 1850s or at some point in the middle. The older the piece the wider the room the seller has to work with.

dealer — a term that has evolved to mean anyone with a tax number that occasionally offers something for sale. There are many times more dealers today than there were 50 years ago but also fewer shops and places to purchase antiques.

dealer's discount — once a professional courtesy extended from one dealer to another to leave some "room" for the next sale. The dealer's discount has become an expectation and a "right" in many eyes rather than a courtesy. Generally, the discount is an almost automatic 10%.

decorator stuff — often a negative term used to describe some of the merchandise at a show that appeals to individuals more concerned with a "look" than authenticity and original condition.

distressed — worn, worked over, showing signs of heavy use and abuse. Shabby chic collectors probably find it especially appealing.

early — a Pez dispenser from 1950 could be described as "early." A Windsor chair from 1750 would be "early" and a Windsor from 1900 would be "late." Everything is relative.

early bird — an individual who pays a premium price to be admitted to an antiques show or market before the general public. A preview party with $69 tickets is a more formal approach to being an "early bird." In addition to early admission, the preview party often involves music, wine, and a buffet.

early paint — close to original paint but one coat later (at least). A piece of furniture that has "early paint" has been overpainted but could easily be a century old (or not).

fake — an item constructed or manufactured to deceive. Not a reproduction which normally does not fool a potential buyer into thinking that it is something that it is not.

find — something that you uncover that has special value to you and is offered for sale for considerably less than you would have anticipated.

flip — a business transaction that usually takes place shortly after an object is purchased. "To flip it" is to buy it, own it briefly, and sell it for profit. Often a "flipped" piece could have been potentially more profitable to hang on to but a quick profit wins out over the long term investment.

glaze — a glass-like surface created on stoneware by placing rock salt in a kiln during the firing process. The "fog" of salt then forms a glaze over the contents of the kiln.

glazed — having to do with glass. A cupboard with a glazed front has glass windows or "lights." Sixteen lights = sixteen glass panels.

Heart — a Febuary country and Americana oriented antiques show held in Nashville that opens with a gala preview on Thursday evening. A national event.

impressed — a marking or decorating technique used to press into the surface of a Shaker rocking chair its size (0 – 7) or the capacity mark of a piece of stoneware or its maker.

incised — a process of decorating pottery where a nail or sharp wire is used to scratch onto the surface of the piece.

MAD — The *Maine Antique Digest* is a monthly newspaper that is a primary source for articles and advertisements about Americana.

married — two pieces that have been joined in such a way to give the false impression that they have been together since they were initially made.

merch — term used by dealers to describe run-of-the-mill items they have for sale. "It's just merch."

"moved around" — a technique sometimes used to deceive. A paint remover is used to loosen the surface and turn the paint back to its original liquid form. That paint is then used to repaint.

"played with" — something has been done to the piece to alter its appearance. It's not original. Restored but not accurately described.

patina — the complexion that the surface possesses that is a function of time, temperature, use, dust, and abuse. A product of its environment.

picked — an antiques or collectibles event that has been shopped by dealers, collectors, or a combination of both prior to the general public.

provenance – a history of ownership. Where has it been? Who owned it?

pool — a technique where a group of individuals agree to not bid against each other at auction. The designated buyer then puts whatever is purchased by the "pool" into a private auction after the legitimate auction. Can significantly hold down competition and potential auction prices.

reserve — the seller at auction puts a minimum selling price on an object that then cannot be sold for less than its reserve. "No reserve" means that the price reached at auction (high or low) is the selling price.

vetted show — an antiques event where a series of "experts" have examined the merchandise for sale and have concluded that the items that remain are as advertised on the price tag.

"right" — an object that is exactly what it appears to be. There is nothing "wrong" about it.

wash — a light coat of paint that allows the natural grain of the wood to show through.

vintage — a relatively new term that collectors and accumulators should be familiar with because it is frequently used. The term refers to a piece that is an earlier example of an item still being made. For example, a "vintage" plastic radio would be from 1950 and not purchased from Restoration Hardware yesterday.

Appendix

Chairs

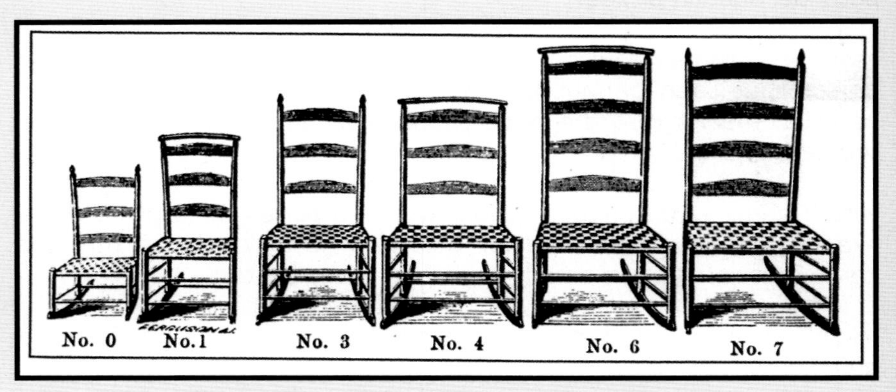

The Mt. Lebanon, New York, production rocking chairs made for the "world."

The Shakers made and marketed rocking chairs in seven sizes primarily from their chair industry in Mt. Lebanon, New York. The chairs were sold in department stores in urban areas and by catalog. The #7 and #4 appear to have been the most popular because they still turn up in the greatest quantities. The #0 and #1 are uncommon with the #3 (a nursing rocking chair) fairly common.

The size of the chair was stamped into the back of the top slat and a decal was placed on the back of a leg. Many of the decals have disappeared over time.

Shaker furniture and chairs were made for the Shaker communities and these pieces rarely surface. The production rocking chairs made for the "world" are still available to collectors.

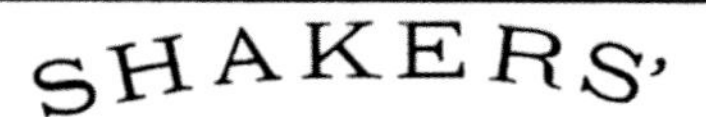

TRADE MARK.

MT. LEBANON, N. Y.

The above Trade-Mark will be attached to every genuine Shaker Chair, and none others are of our make, notwithstanding any claims to the contrary.

NOTICE.

All persons are hereby cautioned not to use or counterfeit our Trade-Mark.

The decal that was placed on the production chairs at Mt. Lebanon. Several eastern chair manufacturers made a chair that closely resembled the Shaker version.

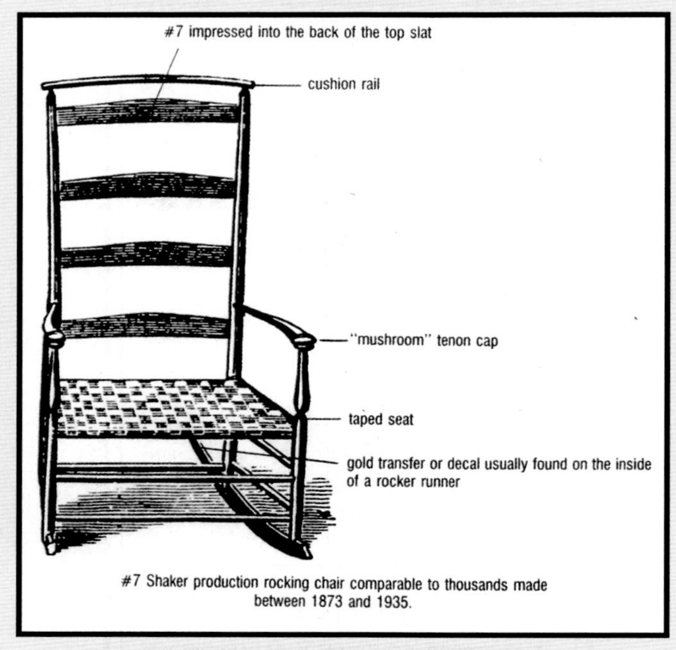

#7 Shaker production rocking chair comparable to thousands made between 1873 and 1935.

#7 Shaker production rocking chair.

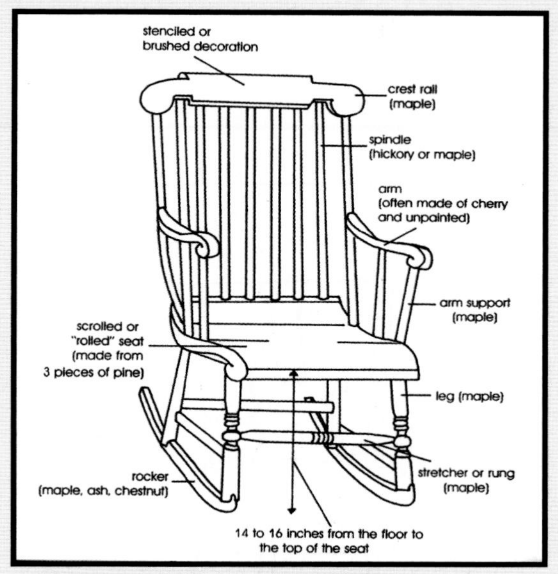

Boston rocking chair, scrolled seat, from about 1870 – 1885.

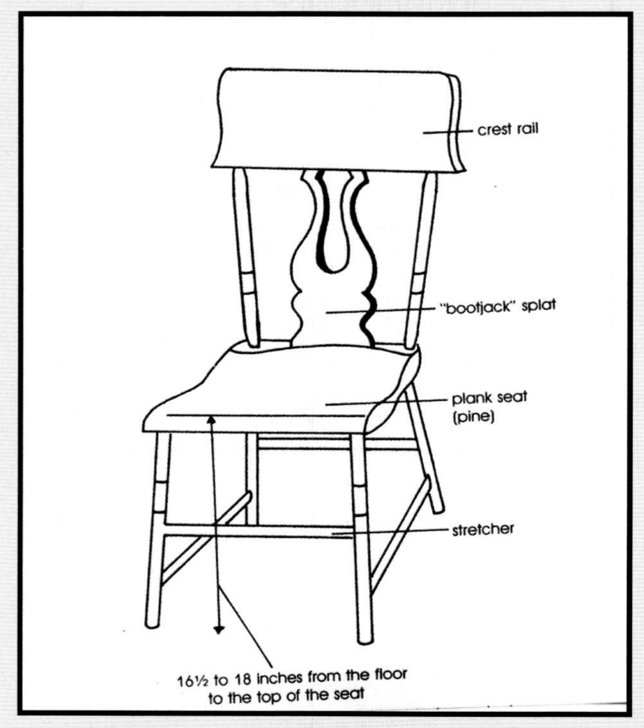

Factory-made kitchen chair sold in sets of 4 – 8 from c. 1850 – 1880.

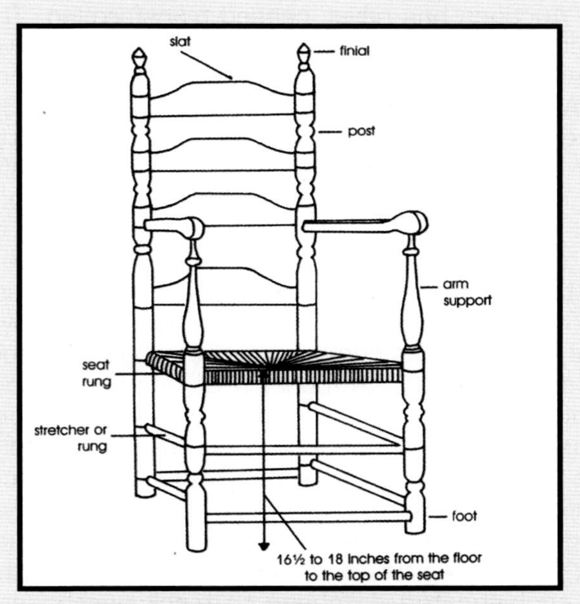

Pennsylvania chair from about 1830.

Auctions

Aumann Auctions

Change, often surprising, is a constant for auction companies. This proves especially true for an auction service such as Aumann Auctions that has been bringing expertise and experience to a wide range of interests in such areas as vintage transportation, real estate and land, antiques, toys, petroliana, and advertising for over 43 years. Technology continues to create broadening possibilities, from print material and web development to online bidding and cataloging. These changes demand an ever-growing pool of talented and skilled individuals to seamlessly blend all these factors, and many more, together to ensure the highest levels of excellence in the auction industry.

Aumann Auctions has never ceased transforming. The company works diligently to help the buyer and the seller receive the most worth and enjoyment out of all the auctions the firm conducts.

Nelson Aumann founded Aumann Auctions in 1962, and the changes he has witnessed in the ensuing years attest to the adaptability that has vaulted his company to the forefront of the auctioning industry. Then, Nelson's full time staff consisted of himself and his wife Karen, and now both come to the office proud to be part of a full-time staff of 17 talented and diverse individuals. A narrow, brick building in downtown Nokomis, Illinois, originally housed the Aumann offices. However, the business grew quickly and now resides in a spacious complex on the outskirts of town. Though the typical auctioneer at the founding of Aumann Auctions seldom traveled more that 15 miles to conduct an auction, Aumann Auctions has now conducted auctions across the United States.

And the tasks involved in conducting those auctions have morphed into a process the auctioneer of a half-century past would hardly recognize. While Nelson's first auction used theme paper and a cigar box for the registry and the cashier stations, the firm now employs a sophisticated database to track purchases, shipping, customers, and sellers. During Aumann's first auctions, buyers seldom traveled more than 20 miles to attend an auction, and so Nelson came to know most everyone's name. Now, buyers are willing to travel hundreds of miles to obtain the needed gem to complete their collection, and Aumann Auctions has learned to accommodate such searches by working to help make travel arrangements and developing media contacts throughout the United States and overseas.

Aumann Auctions has been at the forefront of the innovation that today seems commonplace within the industry. Nelson Aumann was present when the first sound system was installed to the back of a pick-up truck so that the auctioneer's strong voice more easily carried to buyers in the back of the crowd. Aumann Auctions worked closely in conjunction with Internet bidding companies as the technology of live bidding worked out its earliest wrinkles. Aumann Auctions pushes itself to remain at the vanguard of auctioneering technology and improves the industry with its efforts.

It has been a long and wonderful trip for the auction company that started by conducting small auctions around Nokomis, Illinois, and has expanded their expertise to include areas of expertise such as petroliana and other Americana on a national level. Nelson Aumman's first auction sold furniture for a commission of $28 dollars. The company remained determined. By 1981, Aumann Auctions was conducting vintage automobile auctions attracting celebrities and television news crews. By June of 2004, Aumann Auctions conducted a vintage automobile and tractor auction that drew a crowd and performed at a level of which Nelson could hardly dream on that day his voice proudly conducted his first auction.

Change constantly springs around the corner, and Aumann Auctions never tires of the sometimes unexpected lessons the dynamic industry offers. The collecting world expands. The number of specialty interests multiplies. The crowds of buyers and sellers become more diverse. General formulas of success are difficult to find, for each auction is unique, each collection a new personality, and each buyer or seller often a new associate with a personality and a need as individual as the auction itself. This is what fuels Aumann Auctions' innovation and drive. Each day is new, with a new history waiting to be discovered behind each piece they work to bring to the auction block.

Aumann Auctions is proud to contribute a few of the photos and results that compose this book of Americana. The world of auctioneering, and also the world of collecting, holds too much for the interests of any single collector or buyer and Aumann Auctions looks forward to sharing its knowledge with, and learning from, all the individuals who recognize a worth and a history in items from vintage tractors to vintage milk glass. It is a large community indeed, and Aumann Auctions keeps an eye open for that new collection about to emerge around the corner.

Aumann Auctions is ready to hear of it and excited to help bring it to the collecting world. Buyers and sellers interested to discover Aumann Auctions expertise for themselves can contact the firm toll free at 1-888-282-8648, or can visit the company's website at www.aumannauctions.com to scroll through more of the history, the services, and the collections Aumann Auctions works diligently to bring to the collector of any kind.

Auctions

In the past several years we have attended numerous auctions at the Fricker Auction Center (104 E. Center-On Circle Park, LeRoy, Illinois) and been especially impressed with the quality of country store and advertising that has been offered for bid. LeRoy, Illinois, is located on I-74 between Champaign and Bloomington. Catalogs for auctions in the future can be secured by contacting:
Fricker Auctions
P.O. Box 852
Bloomington, IL. 61702
309-663-5828 (telephone)
www.frickerauctions.com

Waasdorp's Stoneware Auctions
If someone is seriously building a quality collection of American decorated stoneware, the primary source would be the periodic auctions of Bruce and Vicki Waasdorp (P.O. Box 434, 10931 Main Street, Clarence, New York 14031, 716-759-2361 telephone, 716-759-2397 fax). The Waasdorps issue lavishly illustrated catalogs for each auction with precise descriptions of each piece consigned to them. The telephone and Internet access bring the auction to your front room and you can bid with absolute certainty. Our experience with the Waasdrops have been nothing but positive. The catalog and its results are also the ultimate price guide for collectors attempting to track current values of a range of stoneware products.

Maine Antiques Digest
One of the primary sources for information for serious collectors of Americana is the *Maine Antique Digest*. The monthly newspaper in multiple sections is currently available for $43 (12 issues) or $79 for two years.
Maine Antiques Digest
P.O. Box 1429
Waldoboro, ME 04572-1429
1-800-752-8521

About the Authors

R. Craig Raycraft is a graduate of Murray State University in Murray, Kentucky. His reality based television series *Protect and Serve* was shown on The Learning Channel and UPN networks. Raycraft's documentary film *The Incident at Kickapoo Creek* has been critically praised. He created the initial website for music legends, the Eagles, and worked with band member Joe Walsh. Travel with the Office of International Criminal Justice has taken him to Cuba, China, Tibet, Burma, Laos, and Cambodia.

He is the co-author, with brother Michael Raycraft, of two books dealing with baseball memorabilia. The book *Baseball Collectibles: 101* is on the recommended list of the National Baseball Hall of Fame in Cooperstown, New York.

Don Raycraft has written more than fifty books about American antiques with wife Carol Raycraft. Dr. Raycraft is a retired educator and owns and manages, with his wife, a large and successful antiques and collectibles show, the 3rd Sunday Market, in Bloomington, Illinois, from May to October.